Partnering with Spirit
Homer's Journey

by Ellie Drew

The story of how a once recalcitrant recipient of unwanted messages evolved into a gifted Spirit Messenger as the result of the gentle yet persistent "pestering" of a man who had recently passed over into Spirit and was himself awakening to his Whole Self.

Partnering with Spirit: Homer's Journey
Copyright © 2003 Ellie Drew.
All rights reserved. No part of this book may be reproduced
in any form without the permission in writing from the
publisher, except by a reviewer who may quote
brief passages for review purposes.

Printed in the United States of America.
ISBN: 0-9743443-1-1

Paperback Edition
First Printing, 2003

Published by the Institute for Conscious Change,
a non-profit organization, which holds the
goal of facilitating spiritual awakening
and personal empowerment through
educational programs.

Institute for Conscious Change
Education for Individual Empowerment
www.ConsciousChange.org

Dedicated to:

Homer and Marge Hefty
who have equally brought bedlam and
profound spiritual erudition into my life.

Those who have loved ones residing in the Spirit Realm,
may these writings bring you peace and hope . . .
remember to pray for them.

Our Collectives, Guardians and the Higher Ones
who patiently guide us and ask that we listen more often . . .
. . . and trust in the Wonder of who we are.

All who seek a conscious Partnering with Spirit
Enjoy your Soul Journeys!

Editorial Note

Less than twelve hours before this was to be shipped for printing I discovered not all the punctuation corrections or typing errors had been saved by my computer. You might be able to imagine my despair after all the hours my editor and I spent on this. Mercury retrograde? Who knows. My wonderful editor, Lilliana Edwards, familiar with the workings of Spirit simply said, "Hum, I wonder what they didn't want changed, or still needs to be done that you haven't put in yet?" What a delight she is to me. The perfectionist in me is cringing, so I am here to make my apologies for those things that didn't get caught in time, or that I'm too incapable of catching - thus the need for an editor.

Within the body of the text itself you will notice there are words I typed in all CAPS, and some words capitalized as Proper Nouns that any other editor would change. I liberally used punctuation as a means to convey what I was receiving, and how I was receiving it, sometimes with very strong emphasis on certain words. If all this were taken out I don't believe you would be able to get as much of a feel for the transmissions as they were happening, and so I left the Homer writings as I received them.

I hadn't read these transmissions since I first received them up until about a week and a half ago when preparing them for print. I'm stunned by the information, and how it all progressed. Having some distance from it has been helpful. I am begining to realize what folks might be getting excited about, because I myself want to read the rest of the information I have that's just sitting in my computer. It is my intention to continue to prepare the next information for print as soon as possible, however, I will not continue these sometimes eighteen hour days to meet a deadline. My kids are telling me I need to shower! That's just bad.

Thank you for your understanding,

Ellie Drew

Contents

Introduction

On 10 April 2003, Homer Hefty made his appearance into my life, but not in the usual way. You see, Homer had died in March, and this was April, twelve days after he left his physical body. He showed up in a prayer circle I belong to; that story is the first chapter of this book. Homer's continued presence in my life, up until his transformation to his Whole Self, 2 June 2003, comprise the rest of the book. It is the story of a modern man many people knew, who studied the metaphysical while in the physical, and made his presence known while in the spiritual, by finding an unexpected opening between the two worlds late one Thursday night.

Partnering with Spirit: Homer's Journey has many purposes and themes, although it never started out that way. It started out as a way for Homer to let his wife and friends know he was okay. For many, this alone seemed like a wonderful and unexpected gift. But as time went on, another purpose emerged as Homer realized the opening he had found with me was staying open, and I could still easily hear him. Homer, and others he began to "network with," wanted to get as much information across as they could in case the opening closed. For two-and-a-half months I'd never had so many headaches from having spirits talking to me - day in and day out - insisting I share their messages.

The rest can be summed up by saying this book emerged into a real life testament to the fits and starts of developing a spirit partnership - documented as it happened, how it happened. This story isn't always pretty, or easy, or clear; it isn't always perfectly said, or without interruption. It is a practical, sometimes raw, discourse of a journey like anyone of us might experience; filled with doubt and wonder, sadness and joy, remembering and accepting, denying and doubting again. Until finally, surrender, humility and compassion, the breaking of the ego and the awakening of spiritual gifts forgotten.

Homer continues to be a presence in my life five months later, even showing up during the final edits of the book, "Clarify this to be . . . ." It

i

has taken me all this time to accept Homer's presence without anxiety about "what people might think." In the following months, from where this book ends, Homer continued to visit me, bring others with him for teaching, encouragement, and of course, to share the information of what I was being shown. Homer began taking me on Soul Journeys (as he later began calling them) into the Inner Realms, lasting two hours or more.

These Soul Journeys were stunning in their revelations, for they unveiled for me how the Bible stories I grew up with really happened but were documented, or assumed to be, experiences that happened in the Physical Realm. I learned to fully understand how our unrealistic expectations of God-experiences came about, and how these expectations have hindered our spiritual development. The mystical teachings of the past were revealed in a way to be touchable and experienced firsthand by anyone of us.

Why teachers of the past have been so cryptic and secretive is beyond me. We could have saved ourselves centuries of work in spiritual development. These are journeys that give meaning to life and make all spiritual teachings universally accessible. Soul Journeys to the Inner Realms were never meant to be hidden, secret initiations, but a natural part of the whole experience of life. Spiritual teachers were meant to openly share and mentor others to have their own experiences. In this way something learned intellectually could be experienced so as to become integrated as soul knowledge.

It is my hope that reading this story will inspire you to initiate your own conscious Partnering with Spirit in a way that works for you. I wish you well on your journey!

Ellie Drew
14 September 2003
Tucson, Arizona

How I knew it was Homer
by Marge Hefty

Homer grew up on a farm in Wisconsin and was always interested in geology, so he obtained a mining engineering degree from the University of Wisconsin in Platteville. From recently going through all his papers and books, I have been reminded of how he was always studying something he found interesting. All his life Homer continued his education in many subjects. It is interesting that metaphysical information about the after life always drew him like a magnet.

After our marriage, we attended Silva Mind Development, took Bible study courses, and eventually discovered the American Society of Dowsers, becoming active in the Tucson Chapter, which helped us develop our intuition. Homer and I became interested in finding water well sites all over southwestern Arizona and did this for many years. We continued our spiritual development with the Nine Gates Mystery School. During the last 15 years, Homer worked with the cubit (based on the Great Pyramid measurements) and made energy rods and walking sticks to increase a person's energy when holding them - verified by dowsing the energy field of the aura. My aura got used to being tested as he perfected his work.

Therefore, when Margaret Mott called me to say that on Thursday, April 10th, she had put my name into a prayer circle (*since Homer had died 12 days before*), it didn't shock me that he showed up or that Ellie was able to communicate with him. In fact, when Ellie added that Homer said he would recharge one of his energy rods because it was getting low on energy (for one of the circle members who attended that night who had purchased one), and that it would be done by the time she got home, I knew this was Homer. Homer had never met Ellie; we didn't know her at all, so I knew that this wasn't made up out of thin air.

Homer also made reference in one of the transmissions to Jesus' quote, "That ye can do greater things than these." This was a quote Homer used many times in his life. Also, "do something even if it is wrong - that is the way you learn" was a common "Homer" saying, with similar ones coming through the Homer writings Ellie was giving me.

In meeting Ellie for the first time in a coffee shop, we were getting acquainted and talking about many things, when Homer came and answered questions through Ellie. I mentioned that he had been in a coma three weeks (medically induced) and I wondered why. Of course, I know that sometimes "why" cannot be answered. Anyhow, he stated he had been out of his body during that time, making preparations to go to the other side. Also, when the time came to die, he wasn't in his body and could hear us talking in the room. Evidently, he was with Charlie (*a mutual friend who was there at the time*) and me when he stopped breathing. I asked him if he had gone to the Light, and he said he hadn't needed to do that. Friends and relatives came to greet him, but "after doing that for awhile it became boring, so everyone went back to what they had been doing." It sounded so "Homer" that, again, I knew it was him.

For the last year before he died, Homer could not walk long distances, and he knew it would help us both to get out and walk in the mornings, at least a mile or more. So I believe it was in June that Ellie called and gave me the message from Homer about walking. Homer had told her that I needed to be in good physical condition to do the work ahead of me. He told me to walk and that he would walk with me. Again, this was information Ellie couldn't have known, and it was truly Homer with a message for me. So we have been walking just about every morning since. In Arizona, during the summer, this makes me get up at 4:30 or 5:00 a.m. to walk while it is cool. Since Homer was the early riser, I have been accusing him of messing with my inner time clock!

I have been giving copies of the Homer writings to many people, one of whom is Gay Luce from the Nine Gates Mystery School (*www.ninegates.com*), who knew Homer and me. Gay came to Tucson to visit with Homer when he was sick and close to going into hospice care, and it meant a lot to him to have her come by. Anyhow, this is what she said after reading the Homer writings.

iv

"There is, of course, excitement on the part of those of us who knew Homer, for there is a light, egoless, yet distinctive personality, with a pixie sense of humor coming through. It is Homer, all right. Free of body and social constraints, he is beginning to offer us wisdom and a map of Spirit on both sides of the veil. It is guidance for becoming more what we were always meant to be - embodiments of light and love. Homer was certainly that in his life. But now, he expresses it as a teacher - a voice he didn't seem to want to assume in his former life. It is such a delight to have his undeniable presence and teaching coming through now at this challenging time, evoking in us the love we have always had for him and for each other."

Carla Woody, an author and close personal friend, even took some of the first Homer writings and included them in her book, *Standing Stark.* In her book Carla went on to say, *"Did I have any doubts that the originator of these messages was indeed Homer? None. How otherwise could particular words and style of speaking that I recognized as Homer's come through a woman who never knew him during his life on the material plane?"*

I wonder sometimes what I would have done if I hadn't had this information from the other side. It has helped me immensely with my grief in knowing there is more to life. We all have a faith to help us through these transitions when someone dies. For me, the messages have been a great help in knowing that there is life after life.

These events have helped many friends, as well as the people in my Hospice Grief Group. I am drawing emotional strength from these stories and hope they will help many others. I know our friends and relatives are wanting to know more.

Marge Hefty
Homer's wife for 38 years.
(Homer was 72 years young when he crossed over.)
11 September 2003

Thank You for Remembering us, Homer!

by Brian E Disbury
American Society of Dowsers
Tucson Chapter

Homer Hefty, an original member of the Tucson Chapter of the American Society of Dowsers (ASD) with his wife Marge, was a quiet, generous, self-assured man, well respected and loved by the dowsing community and other friends. Homer was quiet at times, almost to the point of being inconspicuous, except to those lucky enough to know him and be inspired by his knowledge, dry sense of humor, compassionate counseling and love of life.

Although Homer died in March, 2003, he has not left us, as the love of his many friends allowed a portal to open so he could continue counsel to us with his new-found knowledge of his Whole Self. The presentation of *Partnering with Spirit: Homer's Journey* by Ellie Drew personifies Homer's attributes and his commitment to help his friends realize their full potential as souls while they are still in the third dimension.

The early reluctance of Ellie to participate in these unique conversations supports Homer's own belief that we should always question everything and everybody until we *know* that what is being said has real meaning for us as individuals. Ellie has retained the innocence of the conversations, rather than write a story - which gives real power - for Homer was a person of integrity known personally by many.

We shall all have our own interpretation of which messages are the most important for us, but we are left with the freedom of choice. For me it was reading, *"We should learn how to communicate with our own councils and guides, rather than rely on messages given to us by others."* I was left with a comforting feeling that we are loved, that somebody cares enough to help us learn who we really are . . . . .

I would like to thank Ellie Drew for accepting the responsibility for passing on these messages, in spite of her very busy life, and the way in

vii

which she has recorded the information. We all send our love to Marge Hefty, with our grateful thanks for allowing a lot of personal information to be made available to us by Homer, so we may *all* grow. On a selfish note, we have so much to learn in so little time, I hope the portal stays open a lot longer; however, that may depend on our needs and how much love we can show for Homer so he can continue his communication.

Brian E Disbury, President, Tucson Chapter of ASD.
14 July 2003
Tucson, Arizona

INNER JOURNEY PRAYER
11 June 2003

I call in my guides from the
highest and deepest inner dimensions.

I call in Homer and
all the nature spirits available
to guide me and protect me on the inner journeys.

I call in my most advanced and awakened selves
in all lifetimes here and beyond,
now,
into this moment,
to awaken this stream of consciousness,
living here on the earth, in the milky way galaxy,
third planet from the sun.

I call on all my native and medicine powers.

I call on the Creative Force to help and guide me.

I am ready.

1

How It All Began

10 April 2003

My first contact with Homer began unexpectedly and without fanfare. On Thursday evenings I facilitate a Conscious Change Circle. It could be called a prayer circle, intention circle or manifesting circle. The first hour is spent sharing; in the second hour we create an intention circle, blending our energies by holding hands during a guided meditation. During this time we have two empty chairs, symbolically acknowledging and inviting in the energies of those members who were not able to attend and those unseen to us who might wish to be present. It is our way of acknowledging the unseen world and inviting its presence in for guidance.

We never know what is going to happen during these circles but there is always a lot of laughter. Once a group member was asked, "What do you do in there?" When finding out we were a meditation circle, the young man shook his head and remarked that we sure laughed a lot for a meditation group. We like laughter. It opens us up.

During the meditation we are casual but focused. We might ask for clarification on something someone put into the circle; sometimes we feel unseen visitors are in the room; once in a while someone will get psychic information for another and share it; but most often we simply put into the circle what each of us wants to manifest for ourselves, loved ones and the globe. The group holds each intention with loving thought.

1

Thursday, 10 April 2003 was no different than any other night. We visited for the first hour, shared stories, and started our meditation late. Midway through the meditation someone asked to put a "Marge" into the circle because her husband had recently passed away. As is normal, others continued to add their intentions, but I was distracted by this short, bouncy, enthusiastic, square-ish light at the other end of the table, tapping people on their shoulder, gradually moving closer to me.

I asked about the name of the husband who had passed on because he showed up right when Marge's name was mentioned. I was told, Homer. I asked if he had a bouncy, busy energy about him and six people simultaneously responded with an emphatic "Yes!" I was surprised so many people knew this man. I mentioned that since he was standing here he might want to say something. Everyone respectfully waited.

I could feel Homer's stunned response, "You know I'm here?" he asked immediately. "Yes, of course," I reply telepathically, "would you like to say anything?" I was immediately blasted with an intense energy. It was as if he wanted to make sure he was heard. "I'M ALIVE! TELL THEM I'M ALIVE!" He said this as if he might get only *one* chance to get *one* message through. I relayed the message to the group and then asked Homer telepathically if there was anything else.

Once again he blasted me with intensity, still trying hard to make sure he got through and was understood, acting as if I were psychically deaf - it was a bit overwhelming. He wanted everyone to know that he was going to be at his memorial service and he wanted everyone to really KNOW he was alive and would be there. I saw Homer standing in the front, center left, of a formal church-like setting, dressed in a nice suit wearing a soft pink rose boutonniere on his left lapel. *(Because*

2

the Peace Rose is my favorite and a soft pink color, I wondered if this image was to get my attention or whether it had meaning to his wife, family or friends.)

Homer seemed pleased I passed this information on. We continued our circle. I, like others, continued to add intentions into the circle and yet I was still attuned to Homer. I sensed his mind starting to wander. He was still standing by me but had thoughts of a woman I assumed to be his wife because I saw him sitting on the edge of a bed lovingly and gently stroking the face of an older woman who was clearly in distress, gently talking to her, telling her how much he loved her. He felt sad and helpless. He wanted so badly for her to know he was right there, that he wasn't dead, he wasn't gone; he was right there.

As we continued our circle, Homer's attention came back to me. Out loud I acknowledged that Homer might want to say something else. This time he didn't shout to be heard; he was much quieter, obviously relieved. With gentle gratitude, he acknowledged us, "Thank you. No one has heard me. You're the first ones to hear me and know I'm okay." I relayed the message. He quietly asked me, "Is it okay if I come back?" "Of course," I replied telepathically. I immediately had a funny feeling wash through me, and got the impression he wasn't coming back alone. Homer was making plans.

I did not know Homer or anyone in his family until his wife's name came into our prayer circle and Homer showed up. It is my guess that when Marge's name was mentioned those in the circle who knew them immediately thought of Homer, which may have drawn his attention and presence to us.

3

Addenda

Two days later

Margie Anderson, a woman in our Thursday Circle, called me this morning insisting I write this story down. I hadn't planned to write it up but got such a strong "feeling" with her insistence, I consented to do so. Please understand that I get "information" all the time. If I wrote it all down, I'd never get anything else done. One other thing of coincidence - I received an e-mail notice of Homer's Memorial Service at St. Francis. I never receive these things. I think I might go and see if he really is going to show up in that suit with the pink rose on the lapel.

4 months later

When Homer asked if he could come back and I got that "interesting feeling" that he was "making plans," I had no idea my life was about to change so dramatically. Everything I'm documenting is written as it happens - when it happens. I had no idea what would happen next, if anything. I still have no idea and this is four months later.

2

Homer Wakes Me Up

13 April 2003, Midnight

Note from Ellie: Around midnight, two nights after Homer showed up at our Circle, he woke me up. Before going to bed at night, I meditate and have done so for years and years. Immediately upon sitting down to meditate, my inner Chinese teacher showed up. This was odd, since he shows up rarely to begin with and then only after I've been in deep meditation for nearly an hour or more. On this particular night, this teacher showed up effortlessly, which should have told me something different was going on. He briefly, but urgently, spoke to me about three things to remember - because we didn't have much time. I reviewed these in my mind before going to sleep so I would remember to write them down in the morning.

I went to sleep. Something woke me up. I remember being startled, looked around and saw everything was fine. I went to the bathroom, then remembered the message of my Chinese teacher. Since I was having a hard time remembering only a couple hours later, I thought I'd better go over to my desk and write it down. As soon as I did, I recognized the presence of Homer, and realized it was Homer who woke me up. I could hear his thoughts. And so I started to write down what I was hearing.

"I watch over her when she sleeps." Homer is thinking of Marge, his wife. "I hold her. Tell her I love her. Tell her I'm

5

sorry I had to leave, but I never wanted to leave *her*. I hope she sees me in her dreams.

I'm more comfortable here now. It's not at all like I thought it would be. There are no words I could give you to describe it. It would be like trying to describe God. Words miss the fullness, the completeness, of being here so that any sense of here would be missed. Words are like describing a dot in a painting. Is it part of the painting? Yes, of course, but it is so little, you would never know what the picture was from one dot. And this painting would have to be bigger than the whole world.

Words are like using one grain of sand to describe your whole life experience on earth. It cannot be done. It must be experienced. Understand?

So anything I share is irrelevant for what I know my friends would want to know. 'Details Homer, give us DETAILS.' I can just hear them. What is relevant is that I'm alive. I hoped to be able to come through to give you peace. To let you know I'm okay.

Tell them sound is important. More/as important than light. Do more research on sound sound sound sound sound sound sound . . . . . . Not outer auditory sound but inner sounds. Sound is everywhere here. There you hear a tone or piano key played and you hear one note. Here, there isn't such a thing. The only equivalent would be if the global population were playing in an orchestra. That is one tone here.

Use inner tones for healing. Using the inner tones accesses/brings through healing from here. It will heal sadness, depression, broken bones (break)

(Note: I'm freaking out that I couldn't possibly write down all the diseases Homer was going on about, people would think

6

I was crazy! I stopped writing. However, just because I stopped writing didn't mean Homer stopped talking. I took a deep calming breath and continued to listen in, then write down what I was hearing.)

"How? I can hear you ask this, Charlie, even before you see this. The inner tones heal by focusing your intention like a laser. The key, I think, will be to develop the 'feeling' of each individual you are working on or the issue (healing need) you are dealing with. If an inner tone *feels* right or *feels* wrong *you will feel* right or wrong.

I have to go now. Tell Marge I love her. But she needs to know/accept I'm okay and that I haven't left her.

If you want to see if I can get through to you, *think* of me. Hey, fellas, I'm a good looking guy over here. I'm still a shorty but not so big. And I'm healthy. I'm okay. I'm really okay."

Addendum

4 months later

That was it. It was late when I wrote it and it took up three hand written pages. I heard the name Charlie as clear as a bell; however, I immediately doubted it. I didn't know if Homer or Marge knew any Charlie - I didn't even know Homer or Marge! This was all just crazy.

Women from the Thursday night Circle who knew Marge and Homer Hefty called Marge up to tell her that Homer had shown up with a message that first time. When Homer showed up the second time, Circle member Margie Anderson let Marge know I'd heard from him again. I consented for Margie to give my phone number to Homer's widow in case she wanted to hear

7

the story first hand. One day I got a call. We decided to meet. Two strangers with something in common.

It was two days before Homer's memorial service when I met Marge for the first time. I met her at a coffee shop on Speedway and Country Club in Tucson. As soon as I walked in, I knew who she was. Her energy exactly matched what I experienced when Homer thought of her. We sat down, and I shared with her what had happened in our Circle exactly one week before. Marge told me the only two people with Homer when he crossed over were her and Charlie.

As we visited, Homer showed up unexpectedly. I get a distinct "buzz" when he is around. As Marge would speak, Homer would add to the conversation. For expample, Marge said that Homer had cancer and he wasn't conscious much the last month. But Homer said he wasn't in his body much during the last month and that he'd been preparing on the other side. When his body finally stopped, he wasn't in his body at all, but standing beside Marge - watching. Marge cried, thankful he hadn't been in any pain.

I had been afraid that meeting with Marge would be hard for her. It was very stressful for me because I didn't want to cause her any harm. She had just lost her life-mate, her husband! I was relieved when Marge said she found a lot of comfort in it. I was very relieved this meeting was over and this beautiful woman hadn't thought me crazy. I thought that would be the end of it. I could get on with my life. Little did I know what was yet to come.

3

Homer Is With Others

Introduction

As you read this next section know that for days I had felt the "Homer buzz" and could hear conversations at the periphery of my conscious mind. The 19th was Homer's memorial service, and I felt compelled to go to it. I was shocked to hear much of what I had given to Marge read at the service. I was also shocked to hear people say it was the most comforting aspect of the service.

As I continued to hear the inner peripheral conversation, I had a knowing it was about Homer wanting to continue the conversation - and I was ignoring it because this was not something I wanted to do. I kept saying, "Homer, this is not my second career. Go talk to someone else. You are a dowser for Pete's sake! There has to be someone in your community you can talk to besides me!"

What you read below is the "in the moment" turmoil I was going through at the thought of doing this kind of work. But it is not necessarily in the order I was experiencing it because it had been going on constantly since the night Homer woke me up.

I began having panic attacks for the first time in my life. They began shortly after this third contact when I realized Homer (and others he had made contact with) wouldn't be going away and that this was part of my work in life. People who know me can attest to the scathing things I've said about this kind of work. I always thought people were scamming or I thought people were just tuning into the Collective Unconscious.

I've had lots of psychic experiences, and for some reason those were fine - and brief. But this constant contact? For me to be doing this was, well, shocking beyond belief. So that's how the "Note from Ellie" began. I wrote these notes before, and sometimes after, writing the conversations so I could explain where I was at with it all. Here is my third conscious contact with Homer.

19 April 2003

Note from Ellie: My biggest concerns with doing this is that whatever I write may be taken as gospel truth. What if it's just garbage? What if it is part of an illusion that I'm helping to create? I'm inherently practical. I heard today at Homer's memorial service that both Homer and Marge are very practical and down to earth people. Maybe together this message from Homer will reflect that.

My request to the reader is that you take it all with a grain of salt. Don't take any of what is written here as true. Look at it as the work of my wild imaginings and fiction. That way I can relax and allow the conversation to proceed without pressure to do it "right." What you read - this or anything like it - must be run through your own "truth meter" - through your heart. With that said, I sincerely hope what comes from this conversation helps you in some way.

This man I don't even know, Homer, has come into my life and for some reason I seem to be able to hear him. Or is he thinking of me because I heard him before and he wants to continue the conversation? It is my hope that if I write down the conversations he will stop pestering me!

And it is not just Homer any more. He is with a group of

like-minded people who have joined together on the other side. During my evening walk, I could hear many of them talking to me, trying to make a deal. More like trying to get me to do this when they know I'm the person most *not* wanting to do it. Because I cannot sleep with all this noise in my head, I've decided to simply sit down and write, hoping to clear it. So I'm going to calm myself and type out the conversation as I hear it.

Homer: Finally, we didn't think we'd ever get you to do this.

E: What is it you want to say?

Homer: It isn't only me. I've found a lot of people over here who are trying to find someone to communicate with. There aren't all that many clear channels.

E: What is so important you want to communicate to this side?

Homer: It is the filling of requests from your side for information about this side. There is a greater need there than I ever imagined for meaning to one's life. I had great meaning to my life so I didn't realize the extent of the despair of others living on Earth. What a meaningless waste of your time there. If you only knew how important your life experience is.

I felt in the memorial service today that there is an impression/assumption that somehow I'm in a 'better place' or that this side is more important than the life you are living. That is so wrong, wrong, wrong, wrong. It is equally important. Equally. Do you hear me? Equally important. Don't waste it.

11

Learn all you can. And question question question everything. Break out of normal thinking. Don't care what others think. Think freely. And don't ignore what you get with your intuition. That's us talking to you. You ask ask ask then don't listen. What good is that?

Thought alone we can't hear. We 'hear' emotion. Feeling. Feeling is the wave carrier. Why? Because when you are feeling, you are more present. When you are more present, you are closer to merging with this side and living a fuller life expressing more of yourself.

Now I want to talk about something else. I want to get across as much as I can right now while I'm able to. You are wondering why now. Why can I get across more now? It is because I have so many of you thinking of me now, and it creates an opening for me. As time goes on, so the others here tell me, fewer and fewer people think of me and so there is a smaller and smaller opening to get information through. Many here interested in this work are not able to communicate any longer because there isn't anyone to remember them. There must need to be some kind of carrier frequency (strong emotion and love???) before communication can occur.

E: For now what is the most important thing you want to say?

Homer: That you live according to your beliefs on that side and on this side. At least that is my experience so far. Maybe this is a transition stage where I'm able to do this. Maybe later it won't be like this, but from those I'm talking to here, many of them seem to have been here for a while.

Love yourselves. Love is the greatest thing. It creates the

most beautiful sound. It is everywhere. It is everything. Open to it. I see now that in our ignorance we closed ourselves to love. I'm not talking about physical love. I'm talking about God-Universe love - this all permeating fullness of The One. It is full of Light and Sound. Learn to open to this and many levels of healing will occur.

Trust yourselves more. Make more mistakes. Be willing to make mistakes and learn. You have an opportunity to experience there, so experience it all with joy and gladness, and sorrow and pain. But experience. Don't be afraid of emotional pain. It will help you grow.

Addendum

4 months later

I found when writing, that the conversation would be there and then unexpectedly not be there. Sometimes I would be told that we were finished. Other times the conversation just stopped coming, as if someone had stopped talking.

4

Lightworkers' Mission

20 April 2003, Easter Sunday

Note from Ellie: As I was going to sleep last night more information started to come. The noise has gotten so loud I am back to writing it down this morning. I want the reader to understand how information comes to me. Most of this is direct quotes, as if I'm a secretary performing dictation. Sometimes it's a download of a lot of information/knowing/understanding all at once. Then I have to quickly put into an understandable paragraph all the while information is still coming.

I try to be as clear as I can to get the concept presented across. Also, understand that any "conversation" I have has to go through my own life experience, words and understanding. That means any of this kind of communication is based on my own vocabulary. This is true for any work of this kind. Please use discernment when reading any of this. For now, I go in.

Homer: As I've already stated I am spending time (I'll get into the concept of time in another conversation) with a group of other like-minded spirits here. There seems to be an urgency to get certain information across for those of you on that side to take action on. It has to do with the concept of Lightworkers. From this side, the term 'Lightworker' refers to people who are brighter and their Tone purer, according to their Level of Ignorance. The more ignorant a person, the darker they are, the less Light they have, the more discordant their Tone.

There is a caution here that there are many on your side

15

who say they are teachers of Light but are very dark themselves due to their fear of dealing with their own personal psyche, their perceived mistakes, frustrations, deep hurts and a fear of knowing themselves. The psyche creates a fantasy to deal with the pain, rationalizing it is better than facing their fears.

Living in a New Age fantasy is darkness. Their Tone is off, their Light is off. It isn't that they don't have high ideals, they do. Ultimately all with the desire to be Lightworkers have to embrace their own limitations, face their past, own up to their failures, embrace themselves with forgiveness. In that way they will heal and be true bringers of Light and true carriers of pure Tones.

You call those willing to look at themselves and know themselves Spiritual Warriors - those who have taken up the battle with themselves. It has to do with the self, not work out into the world. The work out into the world is the work of the Light/Sound-workers.

It all starts with becoming a Light/Sound-worker. Pray daily to awaken from your ignorance. Read, read and read. Educate yourselves. Be challenged to learn more about yourselves. Know thyself is your first commandment. You cannot become a Light/Sound-worker until you do. Engage with interesting people that think differently than what is considered normal. That doesn't mean to be irrational or non-discerning, but being expansive.

Get out into life. Be okay with making mistakes. When you do you know you are living the life of the Spiritual Warrior. You have taken up the Sword of Light and used it to face your fears. You then move into the role of Light/Sound-worker where you mentor others to do the same. Your personal journey is deeper within now while continuing your outer journey into diplomacy

16

and healing.

For the Lightworkers in the world, this is the important message from here. Your Mission is very simple, the task itself is not. The Lightworkers Mission is to *Awaken from Ignorance all those in the World.*

How? Education on many levels. Continue with New Thought teachings *and* get out into the world and engage it. Educate about life after death. It is the First Fear. The fear of death holds many back from living fully. Clearly our spirit lives on. Those Medium programs on TV have made great strides for many people with the issue of life beyond death. Much work on this side was done to accomplish those programs. This is one example of our dual partnership.

A primary teaching to have is 'question everything' - even what is being taught here. Challenge people's beliefs, but make sure they have some clear foundation to fall back onto or they will collapse into despair. The foundation is LOVE. Call it what you want, God or whatever, but it is LOVE. The purest and fullest of Tones, the brightest of Light.

Emotional hurt must be addressed. It is the Second Fear. The fear of emotional hurt holds people back from living fully. They need to know LOVE. On this side the emotional hurt people experience works in two ways. For some, it mobilizes or motivates them, for others it collapses them. We see it by how dark or light a person becomes from an experience. Unfortunately some wrap themselves in a self-delusion about who they are, shutting themselves off from the LOVE-Light/ Tones so they have a harder time seeing themselves clearly. Create meditations on LOVE. They shut themselves off from the Light/Tones. It is NOT their natural state - only a self imposed state! This is the illusion. This is the ignorance.

17

Personal experience is more or as important as intellectual knowledge. Create programs with both. Life is a built-in education machine in this way if properly directed. Living life fully creates automatic personal experience. Having the inner knowledge to interpret the experience is the key and primary mission of New Thought Teaching.

Even more important, education should be globally focused. Travel more and interact with the people in the countries you visit. This is in two parts. Some will need to travel to simply break themselves out of their limited thinking. But once that has been accomplished, begin travel programs where you engage and help build communities in other parts of the world. The Middle East is ripe now to have more people awaken from religious indoctrination. For those of you who are called, GO THERE! Get sponsor families and go there.

Creating global personal relationships is the real job of the Light/Sound-workers. That is what will bring global healing. Some of you call it Peace on Earth.

Start global e-mail networks to communicate with others from cultures different from yours.

Sponsor and fund trips for *young people* to engage globally.

E: I'm directed to meditate on LOVE and to create a LOVE meditation.

Note from Ellie: I did a Tarot reading for myself tonight and have never gotten so many Swords. I have difficulty doing this work from an ego point of view - what will people think? Then I remembered the message Homer had about the Sword of Light used to cut away ignorance. My ignorance is to get over caring what others will think.

5

Other Spirits Speak

Introduction

The following conversation was different from others I had with Homer. Out of the blue a message came through in another voice for two friends of mine. When the message was completed - several paragraphs later - Homer continued as if he had never been interrupted.

I was going to edit out those three paragraphs but when I went to do it, it seemed wrong. The information was universal so I decided to leave it. I'm hearing on the Inner Realms as I'm typing this to "leave things alone! It will all serve a purpose." Okay, okay, I will! Also, some of the information was for me personally. I leave it in because it shows how information comes in, and now that I'm rereading this I don't think it was from Homer - only communicated through Homer. You'll see what I mean at the end of this session.

30 April 2003

Note from Ellie: Things have been quiet from Homer while I've been away on travel. However, Homer showed up in my meditation two nights before I was to return home. He informed me he'd been busy networking. I was shown a panel of six people, three on each side of him, ready for questions. Then I was shown a host of "specialists in their field" whom Homer had been getting to know and that he apparently had access to if needed. Homer is like the "host" or "bridge" to information on

19

the other side. For now, I go in and see what he wants.

Homer: Welcome back. I have been busy while you were gone - respecting your travel time, although I felt you check in with me several times. Yes, that was me in your meditation just before coming back to Tucson, and you have stated the information correctly. I am now well networked with people on this side. It is very busy here. I had no idea we were so connected to life on earth.

On earth we live our lives with an inner *feeling* there's more, but we don't know what. This makes us confused about what we can't access so we try to research it, put names to it, play with it but we don't know what it is. Now I know. It is the richness of life that was missing with our ignorance of not knowing that we are so connected to this side. It is like we had cut ourselves off from the fullness of life by not communicating openly with this side.

It isn't only the intellectual knowledge - that's a drop in the ocean. It is missing the MEANING to life that creates the void in people there. That is what causes the suffering, the extreme behavior for people to react. They are looking for MEANING. It is like trying to fill a hollow inside their chests and bellies, knowing there is *something,* just below the surface, but not knowing what that something is. It is the fulness of Light and Sound - the FULLNESS of it - like an orchestra at a crescendo, when the music fills you up. It is like that.

Everyone from there communicates here. Did you know that? Everyone. It is done totally unconsciously for most. Begin a training program for those interested, not in psychic development, but on INNER LISTENING. I will speak more on this at another time.

20

Today I would speak to you on color. Color is, of course, an aspect of light frequency. Alone it is a small part, but an important part of consciousness. Light and feeling are also parts. Why I'm mentioning this is because you can use color in your meditations as a way to more easily access the feeling of Light from here, to make your life fuller.

In schools, begin the day by having children work with color, both visually, and in meditations. DO NOT tell the children or yourselves what the color represents. ALLOW each person to experience what a color FEELS to him or her. It is very individual and must be respected. If you don't respect this people begin to doubt their inner voice, and give outer information more credence. When this happens they lose touch with the Inner Voice. It is the beginning of losing the Inner Connection . . . . . .

E: . . . . I feel dizziness . . . . . a huge burst of energy comes in . . . . In a different voice I firmly hear . . . . .

New Voice: Ellie, you are to do Qigong for Children, for the meditation qualities. That is what you are to do!!!!!!!!!! It is critical. You will get funding for this work. You will have help with this project. More on this another time. Here is a message for your friends in Phoenix.

Third Voice: Hold to your LIGHT and HOPE. You have matured beyond our expectations. Stay focused on your truth. Stay focused on your accomplishments for that is us working with you. We brought you all together - Ellie with you. You are cornerstones but you wonder for what? For life. There are always comings and goings of energies merging, then parting,

21

and new merging, then parting. It is the natural flow to things. There is no need to analyze it; it is simply the natural flowing and movement of energy. It is Shiva, the destroyer, Vishnu, the preserver, and Brahma, the creator. It is the Yin and Yang. It is nature in flow. There is no resisting it. Death creates new life; new life creates death. It is nature's cycle; the way of life.

You wonder now what your current purpose is. Well, to do what you are INSPIRED AND FEELS NATURAL TO DO. It is no more than that. There doesn't have to be any great plan. If you thought there was you would mess it up anyway trying to 'get it right.' This way you flow because you have no choice. Be honest; have fun; do what you get excited about and feels right to you. It is the FEELING you are after - the feeling of rightness.

Have fun. Don't be afraid to make mistakes. Play in the universe and have fun. Deal with the consequences; learn from them. But life never ends. Don't you see? Life never ends. It is only recreated in new ways. You heard today about Ellie talking to Homer; you see, life doesn't end. It is a continuation of life in a new way. So while you are here, do what is meaningful to you. Always do what is most meaningful to you. Then you can't go wrong. When you cross over, you will do what is meaningful to you again. Same - same in a different way. A rose is a rose, but there are many colors.

E: My friends will want to know the significance of their seeing 11:11 on clocks and other things? This happens frequently to them.

Voice to friends: It was when this message was going to come through and you felt the anticipation of it - you were

22

paying attention - it was an easy time for messages to come through. You have received your own messages at the same time besides this one today. There are certain portals that open to make communication easier. This is one for you, but you know what? *When you are open*, there are many more, not only this time. They are open around you all the time. It really is as Ellie stated earlier to you. You are the ONE. The number one is a straight line representing the Taoist Heaven/ Human/ Earth connection. YOU are the connection. YOU are the channel for the heaven energy to express on earth in your own fashion. Do so with Gladness. That is all.

Homer: Now to continue our session about color. It is important to develop these skills with children so they can learn what their inner voice is and learn the Inner Listening Skills necessary for life so it can be a life more fully lived. Create a program of child development for character building and Inner Listening development. One of the exercises is to have the children look into each other's eyes. We will help you with this.

E: And when am I going to get the time to do this? *(Sarcastically)*

Immediately and firmly Homer replies: You must let go of the expectation you are in control of your life. Go with the flow.

E: But what about staying on course until one project is completed?

23

Homer: Yes, it is important to finish your projects, but let us now go into an exercise of what the appropriate projects will be if you are in flow. Don't worry; you are on course and there are many things you've been groomed for over the past years that will all be useful to you now. We have taken into account your personality, which is restless to learn new things. We will make sure your desire to continuously learn and experience new things and new places and new people is fulfilled. Continue with the Qigong for Seniors project. This is good for many. Include a color piece for smoothing the energy. Now about the Children with Qigong. It will flow when the time is right, but that is your next project.

E: Thank you for this information. What about messages for Marge and your friends?

Homer: Today is unusual. This work with you is directed by this Big Being that is standing by me to direct my words with you on these matters. It has a purpose that will conjunct my work with the dowsers and others I know in the metaphysical community. These communities are large and respected. We are all part of a bigger picture that you and I are only small players in. You have the skills for many things to be used to help people that you have been groomed for, just as I have. You have been gifted for doing all this even while denying it. Now stay in the flow and all will be well.

E: I will give it a year. *(I was feeling shattered and defeated to resist this form of communication any longer so I replied with a sigh, committing a year so I could write what I was hearing in my head without resisting it any longer. Not that it did much*

24

good - the headaches were terrible when I resisted.)

Homer sounding relieved: Good enough. Then trust this process.

E: Who is the 'Big Being' directing you? A Guardian? Your Guardian? Your Watcher? Mine? The role?

Homer: I don't know for sure. The energy is very intense, almost forceful. I have to step down the intensity to even 'feel' what is wanted.

E: What is our connection? As in yours and mine.

Homer: A fluke. Timing. Being who you are, being who I am. Common interests. Having common, yet unknown mutual friends and acquaintances.

E: I like Marge. Her energy was exactly as I anticipated it would be after seeing you stroke her face that night.

Homer: Yes, I was lucky in life. She is a grand partner. I feel she knows my presence now and doesn't feel so lonely. We were together many years you know. That creates not only the physical bond, but we are bonded on so many levels. You have seen the streams of bonding for your prayer group and you have only been together one year. We were together many years so the bond is very deep and strong.

E: Do you intend to stay with her?

Homer: Yes, of course. She is part of me. Where else would I go? When I'm here and busy doing what I'm interested in, it is just like going off doing things I was interested when there. But I always go home.

E: I heard music today, beautiful music. Is it from there?

Homer: Yes, that is what is like here all the time. Make mention of the artist you heard so others may get that music and heal from it. It really is healing music. "Music by Marcey" is what it is called. Get yours out and listen again. It has been many years since you listened, but it is a very good representation. (*Marcey Hamm's music is at www.musicbymarcey.com. She's had three near-death experiences.*)

E: Yes, I will, thank you.

Homer: I will go now. You have work to do and so do I. Now that you are back and I have these contacts we will communicate more. On Saturday I will introduce you to people. (*There's a local dowser's meeting happening in Tucson on Saturday. I don't usually attend but will go this month out of respect for Marge.*) Pay attention to those you get a 'feeling' about. I will be there. Give Marge a hug from me. She'll be here soon enough, no need to rush. Tell her to enjoy our friends and family. (*Implied as dowsing family since it is the event Homer was talking about.*)

Addendum

4 months later

By this writing it had been twenty days since Homer first showed up. During the communication I finally gave up fighting and committed to writing for a year, hoping that if I quit resisting, the panic attacks and headaches would go away. Do you have any idea what it does to the personality to be told it isn't in control? And it wasn't only being told that - it was all the conversations going on in my head that I never wrote down.

My head and life had been invaded by the spirit world. I began to feel shattered and definitely out of control of my life and body. I began to give up fighting this because it felt inevitable and resisting it didn't do any good anyway - it only gave me excruciating headaches.

I can tell you it's easy to read someone else's story on this, but to live it is a totally different thing. It is life-changing and I was resisting the change. Most of all I, was resisting how people would see me - as a nut case. You know the saying, "Judge not lest you be judged." Well, I had judged people who do this work in the worst ways. Now, here I was on the other side, experiencing it as a real phenomena and, for the first time in my life, I learned humility, which taught me true compassion.

I was being asked to do the one thing I most did not want to do, and so every day is now lived with humility. By this writing I didn't care anymore what people thought. Some things were of more consideration than worrying about how people were going to see me, such as not having any more panic attacks, or simply having more understanding, humility and compassion for my fellow human beings as well as trying to figure life out.

27

6

Fear & Peace

1 May 2003

Note from Ellie: I'm sleepy and ready for a nap but feel an urgency to sit down and do this. I have no idea what information will come in. I'm just going to open to it.

Homer: Good. I'm glad you are here. I've been busy with many on this side to get organized to work with you. There is so much. First, send my love to Marge and all my friends. I feel their love and support as they read these messages. I'm pleased they are meaningful. Today I want to talk about fear. I have been talking with a man here who researches the effects of fear. It is a terribly debilitating disease of the spirit. It closes one off from the spirit - their own spirit, so Inner Conversation cannot be done.

INNER LISTENING, INNER LISTENING, INNER LISTENING. This must be taught. Life lived in fullness must have this skill or more than 99% of life is missing there. Normal life should have easy access to this side with a free level of conversation going both ways. That is normal. What is not normal is this lack of Inner Communication.

E: How did this occur?

Homer: By FEAR. Fear closes one down. When people are afraid they can't be free with their Light/Tones. Societies

29

and cultures have created such unrealistic expectations that people live in the fear of never living up to those expectations. The Lesson? To cultivate SIMPLICITY.

That doesn't mean not to have means to live by but to live more simply. Truly evaluate what is simple and fulfilled living to what is cultural creation. It is another of the major lessons to teach with Lessons in Truth. Simplicity. This will heal many people's sense of fear. It is fear of not living up to some illusory expectation of success-beauty-relationship-education-fashion-etc.

Next there is someone who studies PEACE. She is quite radiant; she exudes PEACE. I will give you directly to her.

Woman of Peace: Greetings children, sisters, brothers. You could call me the Spirit of Peace, however, I am like you so please do not idealize with unrealisms. I am a seeker of Truth. My interest has been Peace - Inner Peace. I have been observing those who have the energy signature of Peace and applied them to my own life and have come to some conclusions I wish to share.

Not all can experience Peace for it is not in everyone's nature. You must want to cultivate it, just as you develop any skill because you have a strong desire for it. It must be desired above all else. In order to have it you must let go of any external expectations or standards of success, but measure your success according to your own personal and realistic expectations.

Peace-filled people live a life of simplicity and joy, and cultivate the Middle Way. They still suffer from life tragedies, such as losing a loved one, but there is a stillness even in grief. Peace-filled Ones are both withdrawn and active. Some are only able to hold Peace if they do not engage in life but withdraw.

Others are very much involved in life, but hold a center of Peace or stillness. Peace-filled Ones cultivate only certain kinds of friends and associates for long term association.

Peace is a state of consciousness. It is deep within, untouchable, yet felt very profoundly by people around such a One. They tend to create spontaneous healing opportunities when people spend time in their presence. Peace-filled Ones may seem distant and detached, but in truth they feel very deeply. They have taken up the challenge to wrestle their own personal inner demons. The result is Peace.

7

A Dream Visitor

2 May 2003

Note from Ellie: I'm still struggling with doing this. It creates tremendous tension within me, gnawing away in my guts. I can't let it go, I can't relax. It eats at me day and night. I can't get away from it - even in my dreams! Early this morning I had clear and vivid dream in which a large, tall man came to talk to me. His skin was unusually white like it had been painted and he had a very large bald head. It seemed presumptuous that he could show up in my bedroom.

He never looked me in the eye and never spoke verbally. He impressed the words directly to me saying that there were many more things to come I will find even more uncomfortable than writing messages from the Inner Realms; this was only the beginning. He said that Homer and Marge had been together for as far back as anyone could remember, and that Homer and I have done this work before. Homer tended to be the fearless one and I tended to be the one getting killed, which is partly why doing this creates so much stress for me.

Well, I'm still stressed about doing this, but am determined to force myself to have a positive attitude. As a friend of mine said to me yesterday, "Just have fun!" Easy for her to say. Well, I have been directed to sit down to do this work daily, preferably in the morning, something about it helping to get the channels cleared on both sides.

For now I go inward.

Homer: Good, I'm glad you are doing this. I don't know who the man is that showed up in your dream. I'm told here that sometimes these people will show up without any warning. They don't introduce themselves. They are very big and bright. I am getting from people here that it is unusual for these beings to speak to or engage anyone. That he came and spoke so clearly during a time when he knew you would remember is a curiosity for those here, and they are curious to see if there is any more contact.

E: Where do they come from?

Homer: From The Beyond. An area that no one here can penetrate, not yet anyway.

E: I had the feeling he was going to tell me he was from some distant sun or something like that. It was like a peripheral thought, but he knew those messages would totally freak me out since my personal feeling is that all of that is irrelevant to this life. That's when he impressed upon me that what I'm getting now was only the beginning. Almost as if to give me time to let things soak in.

Homer: It is shrugged shoulders here. Or if anyone knows more, I'm not getting it.

E: I keep hearing "Bright Light, Sun Light, Moon Light Heals" in a cadence over and over again. What is this?

Homer: I can't get through easily today with full

thoughts. It seems that the being that showed up is working on you, adjusting your energy - attuning you as you sit there. It is creating a narrow bandwidth to get through and you are receiving only basic thoughts, without the fullness you are used to. It is a temporary thing we are guessing.

Long pause from Homer, then I get an interruption. The clock says 11:11 a.m., if that means anything. After awhile, Homer comes back.

Homer: I've found out more about the man who showed up in your dream. It seems that our relationship is stirring up some interest and we are being observed. Why? No idea, but it is being noted here since it doesn't seem usual. I'm told these beings don't usually have a direct conversation with humans. If I hear more, I will pass it on.

Now about sound. Music played without FEELING has no impact. Charisma in music or voice means that people can be inspired through voice or music because the FULLNESS of the tone is carried. There is a power behind it that can inspire; it can also destroy. Our interest, of course, is to heal and create and inspire so we will look at it in those terms. Some of you interested in this can begin to gather research on sound.

Musicians who are fully engaged in their music will tell you they 'lose themselves' in the music. It is when they are living more fully, being engaged in the FULLNESS of life, as in bridging the dimensions. High states of praise/joy/gratitude/ prayer can move a person to this state also . . . . .

Ellie, I remind you of the Qigong research your friend from California did in China. Talk to him and gather what he has

35

about sounds emitted from the hands of Qigong Healers. *(See Addendum)*

I am interrupted by my kids and unable to continue.

Addendum

After Homer's prompting that day, I was reminded of a time about six years ago when my friend, Richard, and I had a brief conversation about his Qi (energy) emission research. If I remember correctly, I think he mentioned several measurable frequencies emitted from healer's hands; even more that were not measurable by current scientific technology.

When I do the Homer writings, the transmissions don't stay with me more than a couple of days, then I completely forget them. So I didn't think any more about what Homer said, until it was time to edit the information for publication. This means, about a week ago I looked up Richard's Web site, and found the article, *Emitted Qi Training Increases Low Frequency Sound Emission,* by "accident." I didn't even know the article existed. The book goes to print in the morning, and I still hadn't read the article. I figured I'd better do so if I was going to mention it. What a wonderful surprise. It is excellent. I'm glad Homer knew of it. Thanks, Homer!

If you are interested: CHI Institute, San Clemente, California; www.chi.us. Go to CHI Research. Then to the article: *Emitted Qi Training Increases Low Frequency Sound Emission.*

8

Learn to Access This Side

3 May 2003

Note from Ellie: For the past three days I've been utterly exhausted for no apparent reason, but today I awoke feeling wonderful, really wonderful. As I reread some of the past couple of days, I'm thinking it might have been the energy tune-up that was creating the physical exhaustion . . . possibly from doing this work? I don't really know; it is only speculation on my part.

For the first time since starting this, I feel as if I have received grace. I woke up feeling no anxiety or panic at all; nor do I feel sick to my stomach like I have since Homer kept reappearing. What happened? Was it the two beings who showed up - one on Homer's side, the other on my side? All I can say is I am gratefully relieved not to be feeling intense panic in my guts day in and day out like I did for the past month. It is gone as if it never was. Curious.

Does this mean I want to do these writings? No! I would still be much happier if Homer found someone else to talk to. I still suggest this to him, but he ignores it saying it "all has a higher purpose." And if I don't do the writings, I still get terrible headaches. I hope the panic attacks don't come back. For now I'm grateful to feel like myself again. Well, Homer is here so I go in now.

E: Good morning, Homer.

37

Homer: Oh, we are so glad you are here. Did you feel our excitement? We aren't sure what but great things are in the process of happening, and there is a feeling of anticipation and joy. We are being flooded with waves of CELEBRATION. It is hard to put into words. We are being bathed in the waters of LOVE-LIGHT-MUSIC-PEACE and orgasmic climax all at once. It is the best I can describe this.

We don't know where it comes from, but it is coming in waves . . . . . Oh, the music and tones . . . . . Incredible . . . . . Like floating on the waves of bliss healing us . . . . . opening us with no sense of separation in any dimension . . . . . Oh, if only words were adequate to describe this.

It is essential that more of you learn to access this side! This feeling can be felt there, but you must get clear! You must not be afraid to open yourself to your own personal healing. If you don't you sentence yourselves to living your lives in the lowest dungeon of life in self-imposed jail cells. Self-imposed, do you hear me? It is all self-imposed! David, David, free them. It is all self-imposed. *(Rev. David Wilkinson is Homer and Marge's Methodist minister in Tucson.)*

David, there are those wanting to work with you in more intimate ways on this side. Be open during your prayer time. They, too, were ministers on the earth, and would like to work with someone open in that capacity. They will be quite excited to have you consciously work with them. I think you will all benefit from the experience; best of all the congregation will benefit and those you privately minister to.

I am feeling the impact of my words all over the country now. Marge, we are starting something that is having a good effect on people and it is most exciting to continue to have a

38

meaningful life. Awaken All Those Ignorant In the World - this is the Mission. Step by step the intellect must be brought to heel or it will destroy us all.

Love and compassion must rule, but love is not a passive act. Love is an active act. Tough love is the greatest love there is. The *feeling* of love is not love - that is a wandering emotion. You can feel PEACE - that is the true feeling, but it doesn't happen without love.

Love is an action. It is courageous and can seem harsh yet it yields great things. It yields courage, respect, honor. These are great things. The intellect wants only to be clever, to make excuses not to take responsibility for personal actions. It takes love to steer the course. It takes a commitment to love to steer the course. A few days ago I spoke to you about the foundation that was needed for people to have emotional support, and I said the foundation was love. Remember that love is an action. It is not a feeling.

Light & Sound

Now I want to answer some of your questions about sound. Yes, I hear you pondering about it. *(Homer is referring to people who have read the original papers Marge made copies of and passed out. Now that I'm thinking about it, he could also be referring to anyone reading these transmissions right now.)*

E: I'm getting a feeling of Light and Sound pulsing in waves to my eyes. This may be significant although I don't know.

Homer: Yes! You got it. Oh, this is such a good connection.

39

It is so rare.

E: Now I'm getting a pinpoint of light in my left eye, small, open and round with an 'X' in the center - the circle around it and the 'X' in the center are both bright light.

Homer: Light and Sound are the (*I don't have the word*) controllers? of consciousness.

What is the most Light and Sound you receive in modern living? Television, movies, video games! It is critical to have a look at this medium and use critical thinking about the impact of this Light and Sound invasion. There are so many things so say about this. The most obvious is to be wary of what you hear and see in regards to Light and Sound in your movies and television; there is unconscious programing occurring. The emotionally unstable of society could create acts of violence by having more negative Light and Sound stimulation. This is important. Please don't forget this. I only say this as a caution but more I would like to speak to the healing aspects that multimedia awakening tools can have on a society.

The good thing is that if the Lightworker's Mission is to Awaken all those Ignorant in the World, then this could also be our greatest awakening tool. It may be the tool of the 21st century to awaken ignorance and fundamentalist indoctrination.

Light and Sound while engaging the emotions is the KEY!!!!!!!!!!!!!! Light and Sound while engaging the emotions is the KEY!!!!!!!!!!! . . . . Light and sound while engaging the emotions is the KEY!!!!!!!!!!!!! . . . . .

E: I keep hear it repeated and repeated with significant

40

emphasis . . . . over and over again for a long while
. . . . .

Homer: Use Sound as music, Light as colors, and Positive Emotions to inspire greatness.

Concerts have used Light and Sound to great effect. For now I am talking to the musicians. I feel your presence very strongly. Create music that inspires greatness! You as musicians have a great responsibility, because your music affects people in tremendous ways you may not even know. You are also very close to this side when in your creative-zone. There is so much on this side to help you, simply tune into your creative-musical-zone with great focus, and you access this side very easily.

There are many here who would like to help you create music, to do this with you inspiring you from this side, to help carry it to your side. Ask for help and KNOW you are going to get it. Develop rapport with someone on this side in a creative musical partnership. Mozart could hear the music here, and felt he was only able to capture a drop in the ocean of what he was hearing, so you have great help from here.

I would like to see this get printed for the meeting today so I will go now. It is good to see everyone. Thank you all for your support, and love to Marge. We both thank you.

Note from Ellie: At the beginning of this transmission my feelings of wonder were matched on the other side. Interesting. Was I feeling it from the other side and writing about it? Or was I writing this because I feel good today? There is so much to learn yet about how it all works so I'm trying not to make any assumptions, only stating my observations. Is it the inner and outer worlds? Or is it this side of the veil and that side? How

41

are they related? There is so much to learn . . .

Addenda

2 days later

An interesting coincidence is that my Tarot messages and inner messages have been the same. Two days after this transmission I pulled a card from the Osho Zen Tarot deck of a child standing at what appeared to be a locked gate, when, in fact, the gate had an open lock hanging from the chains. The child in the card is looking through the gate, as if he wants to go to a more beautiful other side.

The message from this is card is that we have locked ourselves behind a self-imposed gate, looking to some other side, not realizing the lock isn't even locked. We only think it is. We are to move beyond our illusions by looking within and ignoring that which is external. We are to play with the universe, and not take life so seriously, and go with the flow. Homer could write up his own Tarot deck after what he said about our self-imposed limitations. He sounds pretty Zen-like to me.

4 months later

On the day this was written the Tucson Chapter of dowsers met for their monthly meeting. I don't normally attend these meetings, but Homer had become a regular part of my life, so it made sense to see who his community was. It also gave me an opportunity to pass these writings on to Marge. The most marked thing of the day was feeling the "Homer buzz" off and on.

During the speaker I had an empty chair to my right. In the middle of the presentation I felt the "Homer buzz" get stronger so knew Homer was sitting next to me. We didn't acknowledge each other any more than you would if someone in the physical world would be acknowledged in the middle of a speaker. He didn't stay for the whole presentation because I felt the "buzz" leave after a while.

Then during the luncheon I was talking to various people, when a couple of times I felt the "Homer buzz" come as if to join the conversation then leave it again. When Homer was close, the buzz would be stronger, and as he'd walk away, it would get progressively weaker. At one point I had a vision of the meeting hall having more spirit attendance than physical attendance.

9

A New Voice

4 May 2003

Note from Ellie: I am constantly pestered with a thought, "Meet with Marge and a small group." It's been going on for a couple of weeks. In order for the noise to stop in my head about this topic, I will meet with Marge this afternoon, and a small group she will choose. It is an experiment to see what might happen. This morning I will simply open.

I've changed the name of these writings from Conversations with Homer to Conversations with Others because I don't think this is only a conversation with Homer any longer. At the dowser meeting yesterday I got a very distinct "buzz" when Homer was around that was the same as when he has spoken to me before. I believe this is Homer's energy signal. If that is so, then with whom is this other conversation? It is all very curious, and I don't believe any assumptions should be made.

Centering. Open.

Voice: You are connecting the dots. Homer was and is an opening for us and will continue to help in this communication. He is very enthusiastic, with a great desire to do whatever he can. I/We hear your fear about doing this. You wonder, 'Is is real? Is it just being made up?' I believe you know now from all the things that have happened in your life that this is probably more real than many other illusory experiences people have. What is most real is the truth of opening to this side because we are so

45

much a part of you, and you as a people have shut yourselves off from the fullness of life by denying this connection. For those who want to begin this kind of conversation you (Ellie) need to train them in what you do.

E: Does everyone have the capacity?

Voice: Yes! Do they have the openness is more the question. Heaven/Human/Earth. You have been saying in your workshops that the body is the transformer between the heaven energies and the earth energies and it is! If you are living on the earth, you are a transformer, so everyone has the capacity for this fuller life in partnership with spirit.

E: I think so much confusion has happened because we are trying to get through what is real and what is illusion. How does one gain the discernment to hear the Inner Conversation.

Interruption. Recentering. Open.

Voice: It was the training of the Mystery Schools. You have not been to one, but they are training grounds. Today there are many smaller educational opportunities to learn and grow from, as well as not going anywhere but within. We are the ones who sent you the message to begin teaching Conscious Manifesting. Why? Because you are clear. And you've made certain observations about the nature of enlightenment and didn't get caught up in the illusion of the New Age movement. It also caused you to disregard any experience until it was real to you. This is a good thing. It helped you to be discerning.

We spoke to you a few days ago about Lightworkers. You had inherently known that something was wrong with many teachers but couldn't put your finger on it. Now you are more conscious of what it is. People must begin by healing themselves, but what is the reason to heal if you don't know where you are going? One must be inspired to know where they are going in order to have the strong desire to grow. With you, for example, you refused to do this work unless you knew it would help someone else. Homer volunteered for this as a service to talk to his friends AND to work with us to make conscious contact with you, to get to the moment of awakening to this natural aspect of yourself for more open communication from here.

E: Will I continue my work with Homer?

Voice: Possibly. You will know this afternoon. The group energy will decide. But now you know the difference between the Homer voice/energy and our voice.

E: Why do you say 'our' or 'we?'

Voice: Because we are a collection of voices, many streams of consciousness blending together.

E: Where do we go from here?

Voice: Stay focused and do your work on the Qigong video. It is your work for now. You have work to do and it isn't only to talk to us or we could become a distraction. This is meant to be a partnership, not an end to living your life. Keep up a daily morning time to do this when possible. This will keep the lines of communication open and we can all work together in partnership. We will be there this afternoon. *(The meeting at Marge's.)* That is all for now.

10

In Despair

5 May 2003

Note from Ellie: I haven't slept since about 2:40 a.m. I received a letter from an acupuncture school I'm teaching at that my services are no longer required. I'm okay with that because it was taking a lot of time, but my body is feeling tension around it. It is now 5:48 a.m. and I thought I'd get up and see what comes today (from inner communication) while it is still quiet. I'm sure there are hands of fate around this job termination.

For the past 8 weeks or so my life has been cut up. My True Self looks at it all with a grain of salt, knowing there is more going on than is obvious, but it still hurts. And it was odd how the termination came about; it wasn't logical or what I would expect from the dean of the school. This makes me have a strong suspicion the spirit world has taken some actions to force me into having the time to speak for them by eliminating this job without my say so. I am not pleased with this so I wonder what will come today?

Centering. Open.

Voice: Don't despair. You have been learning important lessons quite painlessly really, but efficiently. You are right about your assessment of this job. In the past eight months in your meditation time, we had been telling you your work was done at this place but you didn't listen. You are very stubborn

49

and willful. There are lessons you have yet to learn, but now you are more open; we needed to break you open. This was an effective way to do this and also free up your time that is now needed. Be grateful to all involved for their unwitting participation in it for you will grow beyond words because of it. In this way you learn to become thankful for all things that happen in your life.

You are very resistant to having conversations with us so today we will speak to the reasons for that. As we spoke to you before it is true that others have not died for this but you have - many times in unpleasant ways leaving behind loved ones in the process. This has created some unconscious anxiety on your part to participate, but it is your natural gift.

We have set up a support group around you. They are all guides for you. Your Thursday night Circle holds space for you. You wonder why. It is because you all have work to do together, of course. They hold space for you and keep you on track. Even Bill. *(See Addendum)* He has been and is one of your guides. He admires you, but in truth, he is one of your guides and mentors.

You see, others appreciate your gifts more than you because they see how rare it is, and also how badly they would like to be dealing with your problems rather that the ones they are dealing with. Your problems seem exciting. They don't know it is exciting only from the outside looking in - but not at all from your side.

E: Okay. I'm talking now. So what! I don't see yet how this conversation is going to help anyone.

Voice: This conversation today isn't to help anyone else, it

50

is to help YOU.

E: How? Why?

Voice: For you to accept your access to the Inner Realms as a normal phenomena will unlock your potential, but you still fight this.

E: I thought I was done fighting.

Voice: No. Not yet.

E: I think I'm fighting because I'm scared. If I do this work, how am I going to pay my bills? It isn't like I want to own the world. Really. I just want to have my little house paid for, and money to pay my bills, and make common sense financial decisions, and be able to travel some.

Voice: In the past when you trusted your inner self, all was provided for you. You lived simply. What is there to fear? And what are you worried about? Did you totally miss what the lesson was when you went to Tibet? *(See Addendum)* Did you so miss it? I thought you were going to give it a year. Trust for one year this guidance. Then see how you feel.

E: Okay. I would like to commit to that, but show me. Please show me . . . . . Is it 'show me then I'll trust' or 'trust then you'll show me?' I have a feeling it is the latter, but you know what? This time I need grace. I'm begging for grace. For once show me I'm safe. Show me I'm cared for. I feel so lonely. It doesn't give me a foundation to jump from and I need a solid

51

foundation to jump from. Please give me that. I need that. I'm scared. I'm lonely.

Voice: Done.

E: 'Done' as in we are done with this session? Or 'done' as in you will show me I'm supported and loved and cared for and will be financially solid.

Voice: All of that, but you must let go of the expectation you are in control of your life. You have a greater responsibility to trust and let go because of your spiritual development. It is your ego, as Bill has said many times, that holds you back. Let go and fall into my hands. You are loved; you are cared for.

E: But I need to FEEL it and KNOW it. Really know it.

Voice: We will not tell you more. You will need to trust.

E: Is this why Bill recently shared his tough lesson of learning 'unconditional trust' with me?

Voice: Yes, it is. Learn from his hard lesson. You learn easily from other's lessons so you get reminders and don't have to experience much pain yourself, for you have already done those things. Now you are in training to remember those lessons. Everything will work out.

E: Well, I want to say thank you, but I don't even feel at the moment I had anything other than a conversation with myself. I know I'm being a crybaby, but hopefully it will be better later today.

Addenda

Bill Wants Me to Channel, and I Say . . .

I met Bill in the late 1980's when in an Edgar Cayce study group in Minnesota. He was a Catholic Deacon at the time, giving metaphysical homilies (short sermons) that were very popular with his church. He was introduced to the metaphysical world through his spiritual mentor, a Catholic nun. Bill is older than me by about 15 years or so and over the years became one of my best friends. He has played many significant roles in my spiritual development since I met him.

In the early 1990's he strongly encouraged me to "channel" information because it was so easy for me to do. This was so revolting to me I told him, "F--- you! Leave me alone! I'd never do that - those people are freaks," and didn't speak to him for months. This gives you an idea of how strongly resistant I was to doing this.

To put this into context I was married to a conservative Ph.D. mechanical engineer, who was getting counseling from our Lutheran minister to "leave me for the sake of the children" because of my new interest in the metaphysical.

The women in my church women's circle were all getting similar counseling with the same minister because in my innocence and excitement about learning about near-death experiences and such I wanted to share it with them. Where else would I share spiritual topics but in my spiritual circle? Needless to say, it put them into spiritual crisis and unknown to me at the time they were all praying for my salvation from the devil.

53

While I was becoming more spiritually free and beginning to understand myself and my gifts for the first time in my life, I was slamming up against my conservative cultural and religious community. It took a while, but eventually I found new communities. It was both a liberating and painful time.

The Tibet Lesson

In the spring of 2002 I received a flyer from a friend who was hosting a Tibet trip in the fall and I immediately knew I was going. Then my logical mind kicked in and said, "And where are you going to come up with $5,000?"

I tried to reason out how to make it happen financially - a smart logical thing to do, of course. I never put myself in debt; that is not an option for how I think about money. I kept trying to figure it out, but it wasn't working, and all I'd hear in my head was, "trust this . . . trust this . . . trust this . . ." I'd say right back, "Trusting isn't going to pay for the trip. Cash is."

After I kept hearing "trust this" I decided to experiment. I decided to see what would happen if I did trust. I had nothing to lose because nothing else was working.

The long and short of it was that over the next months I not only had enough money for the trip, but enough to buy a new computer. It was waiting on my desk for me when I returned home from three weeks in Nepal and Tibet. My lesson? When I'm told to trust, it means get out of my own way and trust. Truthfully, it is easier said than done.

11

Hypnotic States

6 May 2003

Note from Ellie: As of Saturday the physical tension of doing this is no longer there, but the mental tension is still there and I'm dealing with it. My chiropractor has reminded me that my timeline of one year is my ego talking trying to control things. It was a good reminder.

Centering. Open.

Homer: Thank you for offering to do the group on Sunday with Marge. It means much to her and while this was the first time meeting we believe more good things will come from this. The group is not complete yet. Some there will not stay; others will come in. It will be easier to invite those who have a real interest in this kind of thing. The excitement will help in the opening of information. I would remind you now of the primary messages of that day.

People put themselves into hypnotic states. Each organization has a level of hypnotic state, sometimes called agreements. If you are awake at all, these organizations will feel repressive. They are created for people to feel safe. There are some personalities that will work better in these environs, but if you are a free spirit you will choke and feel oppressed. Each organization is created according to the level of spiritual development of each person within the organization. This

57

group meeting with Marge is full of free spirits. It will not be an oppressive group.

It is interesting that on this side people have come across in such strong hypnotic states that they must be brought to deprogramming centers in order to remember who they are. Hypnotic states are not just religious indoctrination, but any kind of indoctrination - social, familial, cultural.

How do you wake up from these states? Ask questions. Ask 'Why?' Ask why, why why even for the most simple things. Some things are done to provide harmony in a society, for example, following the rules of the road. These are not hypnotic states. This is common sense working to create social harmony.

Racism is an example of a hypnotic state. Ask why a person feels that way and she may not be conscious of why. These are the states to wake up from. When you can't answer why or are not willing to look at why something is such a way, or some attitude is such a way, ask why.

Don't assume anything. Ellie is remembering a story of a woman who always cut the ends off her ham. When someone asked her why she did this she said that her mother always did it. When she asked her mother why she always cut the ends off the ham her mother said that her mother had always done it. When asked why she cut off the ends of the ham, grandmother replied that her pan was short and if she didn't the ham wouldn't fit in the pan.

Now this brings up the topic of tradition. Tradition is a ritual. Some rituals serve as reminders of historical significance or to help people enter into certain mental or emotional states. Some traditions are for fun or celebrations of significant life passages, such as entering puberty, or graduation from educational achievements or commitment to a relationship. But some traditions are harmful and no longer serve a society. These are the ones to look at.

The old traditions of celebrating the lunar calendar are the best celebrations. Why? Because it keeps people in the present. Each season has significant relationship to not only the growing season, planting and harvesting season and resting season. These are also reflected in one's life and celebration of these seasons are significant to remind us of where we are in our growth.

Celebrate the solstices and equinoxes. Look up some of the old traditions around these for inspiration in creating your own celebrations. It is true these times hold a time of easier crossover, for you are closer to this side when you celebrate these. Why? Because you are remembering your spiritual connections. You create time to have inner reflection on your life and society as a whole. This is a good thing.

When you live in harmony with the natural energies of the earth and solar system, you are closer to having communion with your inner guidance. Include this in your celebration time. These are the holy days. Not holy as in sacred, religious, but holy as in moving with the rhythms of nature.

David, (*Homer and Marge's Methodist minister in Tucson*) you also have religious celebration. These are also good things. They mark the passages of the spirit - Pentecost, Easter, and others. These are good celebrations. Digging deeper for some historical significance may be a good endeavor for you. I believe you will find that many coincided with natural astrological or solar events.

David, have you been in contact with the inner guidance yet? Beyond your prayer time, it is time now to begin a daily journal as if you are having an inner conversation. There are a host of ministers on this side who would work with you now. You have the capacity to hear them easily. You are to do some significant work with this, if you are willing, that could have a very huge impact on ministers everywhere. How? By accessing this inner contact.

This is the the true role of the Kings. They had this inner contact and ruled from that inner place in perfect partnership with those on the Inner Realms. Listen to your heart. You are in a melting time; the energy around you is melting any resistance within your heart, which makes the inner contact effortless. Begin your journaling now. They are waiting.

Now to get back to hypnotic states. You awaken from them by being willing to ask questions. The day of the intellect ruling is waning and the day of the partnership between the heart and spiritual realm is emerging. The heart center is the holder of the Spark - your connection to consciousness. Mental and emotional create too much illusion. The heart must merge with the spiritual realms to hold in check the emotions and the mental mind chatter. The healthy intellect is right use of will as guided by the spirit. This keeps in check over-emotionalism and mental manipulations.

You could call the book *Partnering with Spirit*. The real message from this side is that the normal way to live is a perfect partnership between the inner world and the outer world and not to get caught up in the messages the outer world is sending. That which is created out of perfect partnership creates healing, support, loving environments, creative works of art and music and spiritual infusion of inspiration. Anything that inspires is from the Spirit. It is kind, playful, joy-filled. To get to those states, however, may require tough love decisions to create healthy boundaries when working with unawakened ones.

60

Now, Ellie, it is time to do your Rainbow Sun Qigong. We inspired you yesterday in your presentation and gave you the Rainbow Sun to work with. It is an exercise that will create great healing. It was inspired from a perfect partnership relationship. Blessings to all. Love to Marge. David, don't forget you have some ministers waiting for you. They are quite ready to begin.

Addendum

4 months later

Here is the whole story about Rainbow Sun Qigong. I was giving a two hour presentation to a cancer support group in Tucson Monday, May 5th, only one day previous to this transmission. The first hour I gave a review of Conscious Manifesting and the second hour Qigong (pronounced chee-gong). But when I moved into standing posture to begin the Qigong my mind went blank. Totally blank.

Here I am in front of an audience and all I can do is stand there. A white space had opened up in my mind and all I could do was be absolutely present without any thought of what to do next. So I guide everyone into either a standing or sitting posture. I literally didn't know what I was going to do next, so figured we'd hang out in our postures centering - that's always good Qigong and not at all unusual to the practice . . . . . After a while I knew the next movement and lead the group, but literally had no idea how long we would do the movement . . . . until the moment I moved into another movement and guided the group into it.

This happened throughout the whole Qigong form, until out of my mouth pops, "Now use the Rainbow Sun to clear your body . . . " It was the first time in my life I'd heard Rainbow Sun

61

in connection to Qigong. When I finished the form people were stunned; it was magical for the whole group. When asked what kind of Qigong it was I simply said, "Rainbow Sun Qigong." This Qigong form came about through this inner partnership with the spirit world - getting out of the way, trusting, and allowing the "white space" of present time to descend.

I had been working on creating a Qigong form for our Qigong for Seniors video project and was two months behind schedule. Donald, my partner in love and business, and working the technical aspect of things, kept asking me when I'd be ready to film. I kept putting him off because it wasn't coming together.

A day after I gave the cancer support group presentation Donald and I were sitting on the couch when he asked me how it went. It was only then I remembered what a magical time I'd had doing Qigong. Why? Because when I've been in the Inner Realms it is not easy to remember things when coming out again. All I remembered was that we had this really fabulous experience together.

When Donald asked me what we did I had to really think about it and go through my mind step by step. When I finished telling him, he said, "Sounds like a good form." It didn't dawn on me this was the Qigong form I'd been waiting for until the moment he said that.

I immediately went into meditation and received the message that this was the form we were to use, but not only for the Seniors project, but for the Qigong for Kids, Qigong for Cancer, and Qigong for Cubicles projects. It was so exciting.

However, in Qigong there are some basic rules - one of them is "never teach a Qigong form unless you have done it for a good long while" so you know how the energies will work

62

within the body. Some forms can create dangerous Qi (energy) deviations if practiced incorrectly and cause real problems. Donald proceeded to say appropriately, "If you're going to teach it you'd better practice it." I already knew.

For the next six weeks I practiced this form up to three times a day. Rainbow Sun Qigong taught me so many things. When you've done Qigong long enough the Qi or energy becomes the teacher. Rainbow Sun began to play with me. Donald and I were so far behind in our production schedule that at six weeks I had to tell the Rainbow Sun it had to settle down into a Qigong form I could teach. The next time I practiced it that day it did, and has become the Qigong form I teach.

When I went back through some of the conversations Homer had with me earlier in our work together, I saw the things he said about color and continuing to work on our Qigong project. I had no idea the two went together.

12

Gifts & Explanations

8 May 2003

Note from Ellie: Yesterday I didn't sit down to write; as a result I felt this strong buzz and my teeth chattered nearly all day. It got worse as the day went on. During my Wednesday evening Qigong class I felt as if I were visibly shaking and by the time class ended my headache was so bad I had to take something for it.

When Homer is close to me the "buzz" is the most intense. Because of this physical reaction and headaches, I've been sitting down to write in the morning. When I do that, the rest of the day is free from buzzing and I can simply get on with my day.

Back to my class last night, Homer showed up with six people. I was also given an image of Homer and me across from each other represented by two circles, one filled in. On the sides between us were curved lines representing three others on each side of us. I feel as if something is missing but haven't received anything more on this.

Centering. Open.

Homer: The flowers are from us, along with the card. *(See Addendum)* We appreciate you being open to doing this and know the past weeks have been difficult for you. It may appear as if we are interfering in your life; however, you have set up your life to be of service. When you do this at the highest spiritual levels you give your life over to the Higher Ones to work through you. They see it as you giving them permission to do what is necessary for the greater good of the whole.

Your whole life experience has been groomed for you to work in this way. Do you remember when you were young and through your teenage years having an inner conversation, and you would say, "Okay, I'm ready for my next lesson." Yes, you remember. The discussion was with us, and we created OPPORTUNITIES for you to grow and learn. You always called us, "Hey you guys."

E: Who are you? Are you my hierarchy? Guardians? Aspects of myself? What?

Other: We Are. And you are a part of the We Are. You are expressing as the I AM on the earth plane; we are expressing as the We Are on the spiritual planes - a Collective that is one. From your perspective it *may* look as if we are guiding you; however, this is not entirely accurate. It is a PARTNERSHIP where there is free choice. Everyone has these partnerships.

E: What is their purpose?

We Are: What is the purpose when it is all parts of a whole? Do you ask your heart what its purpose is? It is part of your whole.

E: But we study the parts to understand the whole. I want to know the parts. I also want to know why Homer is involved with this process.

66

Homer: The visual image I and these others sent you is a representation that creates a circle. I am a volunteer to hold open the channel, give you a contact, and to make the connection so I could communicate there.

E: Is this for real? This feels fuzzy.

Homer: You try too hard. Let it go.

We Are: Inner Partnerships are to help Our expression as You create and bring healing to the people. There are different levels of development for each individual so each partnership will serve a different purpose. One aspect is for learning; one is for teaching. As you learn, you pass it on through sharing. As you learn more, you pass it on. In this way, no matter the development of a person or soul, each person always serves in the role of learning and sharing. Learner / Sharer is better than student / teacher. Relationships are about Partnerships. You learn. You share. So it has always been - on earth and in the spiritual realms.

E: Can or should everyone be able to do this kind of communication?

We Are: YES. However, each person is expressing according to their nature. It is not everyone's nature to DESIRE conscious inner dialog. It is in your nature to desire conscious inner dialog.

E: But I had no idea it would be like this.

We Are: We repeat; it is in your nature. You are always demanding within to have answers - CLEAR answers. You spend hours each day in meditative thought, pondering, asking, following the threads of thought that tie things together. We send you these streams of thought to add to your own so you can learn, but also remember.

It is also your nature to have a strong DESIRE for answers that pertain to issues of the spirit. It is this strong desire that creates the threads of bonding with us. Not everyone had this strong desire. However, the spiritual is ultimately the deep inner longing of every I Am expressing on the earth. When you share this information, it is healing for those who have not yet developed these strong bonds. Share the information. It explains the inner ache and longing much of humanity has. It is a longing for this personal inner dialog.

E: I know people will ask how to develop this inner dialog.

We Are: First - DESIRE it. Above all you must desire it. Above all else.

Second - KNOW it is possible.

Third- DISCIPLINE is necessary. Distractions are easy to come by. Discipline is necessary to practice the skills necessary for open contact.

Fourth - Regular CONTEMPLATION. Journaling / Meditating / Quiet Sitting / Spending time in Nature. Sitting down to do an inner dialog gets you into contact with your We Are. Like in the journaling. Begin to write without knowing what it is you are going to write. In this way you can begin to

68

distinguish your personality from another voice. This is your inner voice.

Fifth - Cultivate an attitude of WONDER. Like that of a child. Remember Jesus said to let the children come to him. A teacher can share only with those open to Wonder like a child. If people are not open to Wonder, they are not open to the Spirit Realms. Wonder at the possibilities of life. This is what makes those with access to the Spirit Realms unique. They still have Wonder.

Interruption.

Addendum

I was given beautiful flowers from one of my Qigong students along with a card she wrote a personal message in. It was very meaningful to me as I was still feeling emotionally beat up from losing my job, and the spiritual crisis I was in because of doing these writings. To receive in this transmission that they were from Homer and friends, through the woman I received them from, meant a lot.

Also the acknowledgment that they had been taking action in my life that created me to be hurt, but explaining why created some healing for me. At least they explained it to me in a way I could understand and accept.

13

The Higher Ones & My Collective

9 May 2003

Note from Ellie: Yesterday I heard a voice in my head say, "Call Kathryn." Kathryn Harwig is a well-known psychic intuitive and author from Minneapolis. I know her through mutual friends and we have a good understanding of each other. Last summer, 2002, Kathryn gave me a reading in which I was yelled at by the Spirit World for 30 minutes solid.

"You are a psychic medium! Why are you not doing this work. It will help many people . . . . . " On and on it went. I threw the tape away, thinking I'd NEVER put psychic medium on my business cards. Ultimately, I decided to accept that it was okay I had psychic moments. As far as I was concerned a very big healing of self-acceptance occurred with admitting that.

Anyway, since I heard the voice say so clearly to "call Kathryn" I did and she actually answered the phone with time to talk, which is rare to say the least. She gave me some great information. It took her four years to deal with her experiences of medium communication, some of which were so negative I'm glad I called her so I can avoid them.

She too had felt that channeled information was simply information coming from someone's higher self . . . . that was until she was contacted. Kathryn said it was a very good thing Homer was my contact because he would act as a "gatekeeper" to keep out unwanted contact and only allow high-level contact to come through. When I told her how scared I was to share this

71

information even when I was being told to do so, she made a very obvious recommendation - choose my audience carefully to stay out of the firing line of those only functioning on the mental level.

The last thing Kathryn said made a lot of sense to me. Recognize that Lightworkers are workers and workers have a chain of command. We are but worker bees. She almost sounded like Homer.

Centering. Open. I feel this intense "buzz" which is an indication that I am making contact with Homer.

Homer: We have sent you many personal messages of support and people to support you to make this transition easier. The woman who called you just now was guided to call you so you could hear her feelings about the channeled information Emmanuel sent through. Yes, the information we are working with will be healing and we will continue to show you this. Relax and trust us.

E: I'm afraid I'll get burned. What if I trust this and end up getting crucified? I don't want to be any religious right-wing target. It is too hurtful.

Homer: That is why you were born with a Leo Mars. It will give you courageous action. It is also why your Venus and Mars are within one degree of each other. Your actions can only reflect your heart. People will recognize this if they are open because they will feel it.

Now today we wish to talk to you about Spirit. The spirit resides within the body. The body is temporary but while living on earth it may feel like the be all, end all of existence. It is not.

72

It is temporary. But while there you must take advantage of all you can and make the most of your time. The best way to do this is to develop your Inner Listening Skills.

Each of you has a Council. It is the best word I can use. They are made up of Spirits at the same developmental level you are. They grow with you as you do your work. How you engage life is not only for you alone, but for you and your Council. The Council has not lost their memory of who they are. They can give you guidance, and for the most part, it can be trusted. This guidance is felt within your body. There is someone else who wishes to speak about this now:

The Higher Ones

Being of Power: (Very Bright and the energy signature is very intense.) Homer has not been here long enough to explain the hierarchy. I am from the Higher Council and will explain. A group of beings make up a Collective. One, or sometimes more than one, within the Collective will chose to incarnate on the earth. They support each other just as friends will. These are friends on the Inner Realms.

Each Collective has more experienced Guardians. They are like big brothers and sisters to mentor your Collective, watch over and, well, like a good guardian and mentor, keep you out of trouble if you start to stray too far out of purpose.

In the beginning new souls within the Collective begin to mature and a cry within becomes, 'Is there more? There must be more.' When this desire reaches a certain pitch it garners the attention of the Higher Realms - the Spiritual Realms - and this is when the real work begins to happen in a person's life and the Collective's life.

The Collective *and* the incarnated one from within the

73

Collective begin to be influenced by the healing tones of the God Force and reach the beginning stages of consciousness. Yes, we are sending you these waves of Light and Sound now. And you feel the activation happening within your head and the feeling of it filter down though your body.

These waves of Light and Sound open and clear the entire Collective, the one incarnated and the ones within the Collective staying on this side. The Sound and Light are washing through your Open Spaces creating an expansive feeling within you. The Sound clears the Open Spaces and begins to free the souls within the Collective. Sit with it a moment and report what it feels like.

E: Expansive . . . . . Pressure in the head . . . . . Internal bright light . . . . . Open feeling. I hear music, pulsating music . . . . . physically I feel a bit numb. Oh, I see someone. Yes. . . . . Oh, more than one now.

New Voice: *(See Addendum)* We are the Higher Ones. We no longer incarnate, but have passed through the lower stages. We express to the Collective as Inspiration and Wonder. We often do this through Music, Tones, Chimes, Bells, Birds, Wind - that which represents freedom of flight. It is the freedom of your Spirit to soar.

E: What good does this do us?

Higher One: This contact gives you a sense of meaning to your life. Purposefulness. We are the Inner Inspiration. We express as the planets of Neptune and Uranus and Venus and Mars. The One (God), Freedom, Love and Action.

Without this life is meaningless and you would only live

according to the animal hormonal instinct programmed into the species. This contact is what makes the homo sapian human, as it continues to develop into a higher level being. Not all have achieved this. Some are clearly still living instinctually, but it is everyone's purpose to achieve this.

E: Why?

Higher One: To experience. To push the bounds of creation itself. However, earth is the school to graduate from. To learn the Lessons of Inspiration. To appreciate the Lessons of Inspiration and desire it above else. Inspiration is Light and Sound. Once this is achieved and cultivated you no longer want to experience within the earth realm because you will have graduated into the Higher Realms.

There are those who choose to go back, of course, to help the rest of their Collective achieve this and experience this, and sometimes a whole graduated Collective will go back to be Spiritual Teachers. Earth can be a very hostile place, but the Lightworkers choose to go back as teachers. Their work is done quietly often times as schoolteachers.

The children is where to spend all the time and energy and financial resources. It is with the children. The whole planet would jump in consciousness if all the resources of the planet were put to benefit children. This is the cause of so much disharmony on earth. The children are being sacrificed for global economic development.

You all come in as children. If you were nurtured in your creativity, inspired with art and music, meditation and play you would develop quickly. Character building, honoring the spirit, and emotional support is what is needed. Then the planet would evolve quickly.

75

Put all your resources to the children. Love them. Support them. Children before the age of puberty must have access to the arts and character development so when puberty and animal instinct kick in they have a solid foundation to use their aggressive hormonal action to perpetuate that which inspires. As they become adults, they will take actions that will perpetuate the arts and music. And most important, they will become leaders and policy makers of integrity so the earth and its children are not destroyed.

Do what you can to nurture the children. For every child born there is a Collective left behind that is learning from their experience. Even on this side there would be great growth and development. Choices made on either side effect the other. Make more choices for the children.

Here is a Collective's Guardian/Mentor. *(The feeling is androgynous, gentle and loving in feel)*

Gardian: Be free. I wish to give you a list of thing to teach the children. It was We who gave you the directive through Homer to begin a Qigong for Children Training Program. We will participate with you on this project. Stick with it. Do not despair.

Children must find their Inner Freedom. Create visualizations for them to explore their creative expressive sides. Encourage anything in the arts and music, respect, character building, honor, discipline, play. Experiment with sound to calm them.

E: . . . . . . I'm not getting anything clear right now . . . . .

My Collective

Homer: You held their intensity for a long time. It is difficult even for me to endure their intense Light and Sound.

I believe they will speak with you again. This experiences is a good start. It is my feeling there will be some who read this that will know exactly what their work is. The message was to activate certain memories within yourself and others who read this. Please share it. Your Collective would like to speak now.

Collective: Greetings. Yes, we are your "Hey You Guys." You never lost contact with us though your life. You just forgot on a conscious level whom you were talking to.

E: I see six of you.

Collective: Yes. You have always asked us if you were ready for your next lesson, and you haven't asked in a while so we sent it to you anyway because it was time to have this conscious contact. Homer has been a great friend and help and has make this possible.

E: Is it true that some have very negative experiences when doing this? I don't want to be psychically attached.

Collective: We sent you Kathi Cavanagh. *(Chapter 14)* She and her personal Collective hold some guardianship for you. Your thoughts are also very powerful; when you called on the the 'Guardians to guard' it was they along with your own powerful Light/Sound. You are very powerful in your own right.

You have gone back there to be a teacher/messenger. Even though you find this type of communication very natural you have strongly resisted it. You have resisted it because you are living in the cultural energy matrix of a warped sense of success. It affects everyone in Western society to some degree. And spiritual matters are not a part of being successful to the outside world. The spiritual ones who are awake and chooses positions

77

of power bring this spiritually awakened state with them. We need more of this.

But all that aside, your mission is now in the early stages of unfolding. With this conscious contact we will guide you to help many people. We will give you our guidance as we are guided through our contact with the Higher Ones. We are guided by them and in contact with them at all times.

Our energy has been attuned so their intensity does not harm us and we will pass that information on to you unless they wish to impart it to you directly. They do not wish to harm you. The purpose of having direct contact with the Higher Ones now was so you would have first hand experience of them and know their energy signal.

Contact Your Collective

E: I know others will want to know how to contact their own Collectives . . . . .

I see discussion within the group occurring . . . . . no words, but a picture/visual. I'll do my best here. It looks like entering through an arch of a really big underground overpass into a garden/park with many milling about.

E: Can people access their collective through this visualization?

Collective: Yes, one way is to visualize walking through a tunnel to a park with intention to meet their Collective. It is for the individual to go to the beings who *feel* familiar.

E: Okay. So we have an inner Collective who has Guardians who are in contact with the Higher Ones.

Collective: The Higher Ones can both mentor the Guardians and move on. The Higher Ones are also part of a Collective who have experiences within other Light/Sound schools.

E: I'm sensing a world that is all music . . . . there is nothing but music and tones.

Collective: Yes, we are merging with The One in the dance of creation itself. It is a very joyful experience.

E: Why do you say this? It is as if you have done this.

Collective: (Laughter) How do you think you were able to manifest so easily in 1978? You/We were accessing this connection with The One.

E: But how could I do this and be here?

Collective: Were you there? You may have had a small part of yourself there, but remember you spent hours in meditation and bliss and wonder. During the night you were not there at all except for your physical shell. You had been dancing with The One.

E: But I thought that in order to dance with The One you had to graduate from Earth.

Collective: We Have! We choose to come back as teachers, but that doesn't mean you lost the ability to access your dance with The One. Your personality is confused, that is your body-hormonal-animal-human aspect. It is really a very small part of you.

E: But isn't everyone's one life like this?

79

Collective: No. They are not. Do they have the potential? Yes, of course, and one day they will master their lessons but no, not everyone is like this who is on earth. That is why the teachers come back.

E: But I'm NOT different than others here. I know this.

Collective: You only think this. It is your ego speaking, your personality. Bill has been trying to tell you for years that you were different. Many others have been telling you you were different. You are different. Not that you are better than anyone else, we had to go though our lessons too, but you are not a beginner there. We have done many lifetimes of lessons to achieve liberation. You are still liberating yourself from your immersion there, but your spirit is free and knows it. Your personality is just now waking up.

E: Okay, if I'm honest I've felt as if I have always known things but couldn't remember. Is this contact what I forgot?

Collective: Yes.

E: What is my purpose for being here?

Collective: To teach.

E: And to learn?

Collective: Yes of course, we are always learning.

E: Am I to bridge the Spirit Realm with the Earth Realm?

Collective: Yes, we have been sending you images and words of 'bridging' for months now.

E: Now that I've made contact with you directly will

80

Homer still be my contact?

Collective: Yes, until he chooses differently. But he is enjoying this work, and he is learning from this also. He will have his own messages to pass on.

E: I'm very tired, I will go now. Thank you for answering my questions.

Collective: Blessed Be.

E: Wait a minute. That sounds like a Wiccan saying. I haven't read anything about them and don't know anything about them except I've heard this saying while watching Buffy. (Television program, *Buffy: The Vampire Slayer*) Why did you end our session with this?

Collective: It was appropriate. Not for you, but for someone else who will be reading this. They will know.

E: Why do I get the feeling I've fallen down the hole in Alice in Wonderland?

Collective: (Laughter) Life isn't as it seems. That is all.

Addendum

4 months later

In this session I felt the "Homer buzz" but all the rest who communicated with me had their own distinct feel to them - like a motor that runs from a low to high pitched hum when it is running differently.

When the Higher Ones came in it was literally as if all the energy from a huge stadium light had honed down to a one inch

81

beam and focused at my third eye area. I was feeling my brain fry and realized this is what it must have been like when mystics of the past ended up in looney hospitals when they spent too much time in this energy.

It was so intense that when they stopped my head jerked back as if released from something. I remember thinking at the time that if this is what I was in for, well get a room ready for me because I wouldn't be mentally intact for long. I'm glad they don't come often. When asking my Collective why they came in I thought it funny when they implied I wouldn't believe them if they only told me about the Higher Ones. Now I'd had my own experience so knew the reality of such ones.

This session was a wonderful revelation for me in other ways. For the first time in my life I actually knew and could consciously communicate with "Hey You Guys" and knew they were my Collective. The past couple of sessions with Homer made sense to me now with the six he showed up with. Hindsight is great, but in the moment how could I have known?

When I finally figured it out I felt as if I were pretty dense not to pick up the fact that "Hey You Guys" were the same as my Collective sooner than I did. Sometimes what is right in front of our face can't be recognized without having a framework to put it into. For the first time I understood the Native American story about the Indians not seeing a ship in their harbor until they were taken aboard because they'd never seen one before.

14

Blue Light Experience

Thirteen months and two days before Homer

Note from Ellie: This information had originally been an addendum to the previous chapter, however, due to its length and the significance of the experience I have added this chapter. I believe this event was the beginning of setting up my communication with Homer thirteen months and two days later.

8 March 2002

Kathi Cavanagh is a woman I met in my healing practice in Minneapolis and we immediately bonded, as if we'd always known each other. One day I heard a voice say, "Ask Kathi and her meditation group to hold protection for you and your teachings. She is to be your guardian." I called her up to share what I'd heard and ask if she would be willing to do this. "Of course!" she said. From that point forward I felt a difference in the energy around me.

One event of her holding guardianship for me was so bizarre as to be almost impossible to explained by rationality. I was in Yuma, Arizona giving a weekend workshop on Conscious Manifesting and Qigong for some doctors and nurses. After teaching Friday night I went back to the guest house I was staying at, which was surrounded by ten acres of blooming orange trees. It was exquisite.

That night, while settling into meditation, I had come to two

83

decisions I was ready to act on. For the past nine months I'd been hearing a voice say to me, "It is time for you to communicate with us more consciously." I heard this almost constantly and my reply was always the same, "No, thank you. How I communicate now is just fine. I already get more information than I know what to do with. I don't want or need more of this." But now something had changed within me.

That day I had decided to let go and trust about going to Tibet. On a whim I decided as long as I was going to let "them" know that, I'd also let go and changed my stance on the voice who kept saying, "It is time for more conscious communication with us" to "okay" instead of my usual "no, thank you." I settled into the mediation, centered and stated, "I am open to going to Tibet, provided the money is available, and I'm finally open to more conscious communication with you."

Immediately the most stunning thing happened to me. I felt like the Batman car being armored, with a sectioned shield going up my back and separate sections to my right, left, in front, above and below me. In an instant I had an open metal framework around me. I thought, "Well, okay . . . . . this is an interesting way to say hello." I found it odd I didn't feel anything.

Then I heard whispering above me. I looked up and saw an open, wide circle of white light about twenty feet above me. I focused on the whispering and heard, "The Light descends, the Light descends, the Light descends" repeated over and over by thousands of voices. In the midst of those whispers I heard a few, "The Christ Light descends." I had no idea what this meant.

I noticed a couple of other things, too. I was able to see both outside myself while also staying in the experience of what was

84

happening. My observer-self saw my experiencing-self about fifteen-feet tall instead of my physical five-feet-two inches.

All of a sudden I sensed a change. In the midst of the whispering I began to see a Light descending through the opening of the white light circle. It was an immense Blue Light in the shape of a marquise diamond, descending exactly from above me. I realized it was going to descend right where I was standing within this metal framework, and I couldn't do anything about it.

I started to panic, but realized as it descended I didn't feel a thing. It continued down until it snapped into place within the metal framework; I just happened to be in the middle of the framework. I still found it odd I didn't feel anything.

The next thing I knew I felt a burning in the middle of my back, directly behind my heart center at the spine. I looked with my observer-self and saw a large blue dragonfly man with the tail end of his abdominal segment stuck into my back where it hurt. I said, "Hey, knock it off. That hurts!" He immediately left; however, my feeling was that he was done with whatever he was doing anyway.

From the front I noticed two smaller blue dragonfly men within the Blue Light and received a knowing they were technicians "making adjustments," and I was not to mess with them. I couldn't even if I wanted to. I received a knowing the reason I didn't feel the framework or Blue Light was because they were slightly out of phase with my physical body. That was about to change.

In an instant three things happened simultaneously; they took only the briefest moment to complete. First, a wave of dizziness washed over me and I began to lose consciousness, while feeling every cell in my body begin to change. Second, I

85

had a strong knowing that I was terribly vulnerable during this phase of aligning the Blue Light with my physical body, because I felt/heard the concern of those working on me.

And last, immediately upon the alignment starting, I saw darkness moving at tremendous speeds coming at me, looking like a camera lens closing fast. I knew, without a doubt in my mind I was in danger, so I did the only thing I could think of. I firmly called out, "Guardians, guard!" The last thing I saw before fully losing consciousness was four people standing in the four directions with their hands out, holding the blackness at bay outside the ring of light.

The next morning I awoke and didn't remember anything. I thought the bed had been comfortable, but my upper back was in extreme pain. No matter what I did I couldn't get it to loosen up so I took an Ibuprofen and left to teach all day.

On my way back to the guest house that night I decided to call home, and was forced to stop by an open field because my cell phone wouldn't work if I went further. It was dusk and I remember seeing three owls that kept circling my car instead of chasing the rabbits in the field. They would land and I could feel them staring at me then fly circles again. I remember remarking about this to Donald when he said, "Kathi Cavanagh called a few minutes ago." I hadn't talked to Kathi for months but figured as long as I had free cell phone minutes, I'd give her a call.

"Hi, Kathi, I heard you just called." "Hi, Ellie . . . what a coincidence, but I didn't call you, it must have been someone else. This is so weird. I was literally reaching my hand across the desk to call you when the phone rang and here it is you! I have something to tell you about what happened last night."

As soon as Kathi said this, I felt a flood of warmth infuse my body, and I instantly remembered everything that happened the

86

night before. "Yeah, me too." I let Kathi talk first. Here is her story as I remember it.

For years Kathi has met with her meditation group of three women and a man, each of whom hold a direction. They know they were guided to work together and so meet regularly once a month. Kathi hadn't been able to attend for awhile because she had started a second job putting on home demonstrations with a food company. Friday, 8 March 2002, was no different, or so she thought. As it turned out an unusual series of bizarre coincidences happened to each of the people planning to attend the event, forcing the hostess to cancel.

That night Kathi was able to attend the meditation group for the first time in months. When the four gathered all were antsy, each remarking on how they could hardly wait to gather that night. They were all feeling like "something important was going on" and "I feel it, it's big, but what is it?" And, "We don't know, but we all feel an urgency, and it was important to gather. Look at what happened so Kathi could be here. So let's not talk any more. Let's go in and see."

I asked Kathi what happened, and she reported that they had all felt tremendous amounts of energy, like they'd been busy doing "something," but no one could say what. Everyone had felt it had been important they were all together and they trusted they did what was needed even if they weren't conscious of it.

Then Kathi said the most remarkable thing to me. "Ellie, the oddest thing was when we came out of the meditation all our hands were burning. They all looked the same - bright red as if our hands had been brushed with red paint or fresh blood. It took a while for the burning to stop."

I asked her, "What time were you doing this last night?" It was exactly when I had been in my meditation time - two time

87

zones apart - without any contact with Kathi in months. I said, "Ah, Kathi, you want to know what you guys were doing last night?"

Over the course of the next fourty days nothing happened. Nothing in my meditation time. Nothing psychically. No voices. Nothing, absolutely nothing, only silence. Then one morning I hear a voice as clear as a bell, "Go into meditation." I shrugged my shoulders and thought, "Okay. Morning isn't my usual time to do this, but okay."

Immediately upon closing my eyes I was immersed in the Blue Light. I was taken straight up into it, and handed a dark blue velvet bag tied with a string. It was decorated with gems and pearls. Out of curiosity I opened it thinking, "Yeah! Maybe it's fairy dust." I was very disappointed, however. It was a grey- blue powder that looked like fine concrete dust. It didn't shine or sparkle at all, and it looked very boring. I was rather disappointed. Then I was in my room again. I looked at the time and an hour had passed.

There is more to this story, but no time for all of that now. I did want to share one of the key experiences that relates this to Homer. After a couple more Blue Light meditation experiences I was told to go into two weeks of prayer, fasting and meditation. This was summer 2002. During that period I was guided when to meditate, read, sleep, journal and drink miso broth.

I was told to document the full two week period, which I did. It was at that time "they" trained me to stay in a shamanic state while journaling, recording my experiences. When I was able to Soul Journey and record it while typing at my computer, I was abruptly told my lessons were complete, and my fast was over. When Homer showed up, it was easy to document what he was saying.

15

I Almost Walk Away

10 May 2003

Note from Ellie: I'm beginning to understand the different visceral messages to the different energy signatures from whomever is coming in. Homer is a "buzz" where my teeth feel like chattering. My Collective is very familiar and like smooth honey and home. The Higher Ones are a bright invasive light with intense power to the frontal lobes of my brain felt as pressure at my forehead. I thought I'd clean the house today, but the buzz has started so I'll sit down to type. Who knows what will be said today.

Centering. Open.

Homer: The Higher Ones wish to speak today. You are being attuned.

Higher One: Yesterday you were fully integrated and your memory was fully awakened to your Collective. Today we wish to fully integrate you and awaken you from your slumber of our Higher Connection. You are one of us, functioning with an earth Collective and within this Higher Level Collective. And even beyond this. Many living on the earth right now are these multidimensional beings living in many dimensions at once.

E: What is the purpose of doing this?

Higher One: Our mission is to awaken our creation into

consciousness.

E: Our creation?

Higher One: Yes. We are constantly creating new worlds and infusing them with our energy. You are very much involved with the Fairy Kingdom. You have always known about them, but your earth mind has rationalized them as being only fairy tale. They are not. And many other creations of thought are not fairy tale.

E: What about the negative forces?

Higher One: There are forces of darkness that have gotten created. These creations are created from ones who were semiconscious and didn't know their manifesting power.

E: Can they be un-created?

Higher One: They can be un-created if done so early in the development.

E: I'm not comfortable speaking of this. It sounds hocus pocus. My agreement was to speak of helpful things to people living here on the earth. What can you tell me that will be helpful for people here so they may develop and grow?

Homer: We've lost the connection. You are holding on too tight. When things are said that your mind cannot yet handle it closes off the connection.

Addendum

4 months later

I remember this session being extremely tense for me, and I was glad when I lost the connection. I closed my computer and walked away, sure I'd never be back. Being part of creating the Fairy Kingdom? Ha! I remember saying to Homer one day that I refused to write any New Age bullshit and he immediately replied, "Good" and then proceeded with whatever he was telling me.

16

The Fifth Mind

11 May 2003, Mother's Day

Centering. Open.

E: What messages are there today?

Homer: Happy Mother's Day. You, Marge and other's will help in birthing inspiration for many around the world. I know you don't believe this, but as I have stated before, we are only instruments in a much larger picture. You wonder what that larger picture is. It is the remembering of not only who you are but who all of us are who are reading/hearing this information.

For those of you reading this, you are awake enough to understand that you've always had Inner Knowing, while at the same time wondering what it is you've forgotten. Those of you reading/hearing this are graduates of the earth. Yes, the graduates.

An aspect of yourself has come back to be teachers. You have come back to be the instruments through which this world may be liberated. Many of you have forgotten all together what your purpose is because of the day to day drudgery of doing labor to make bill payments. Awaken now into remembrance. We are a joyful lot, dancing within creation itself. Everything is in perfect flow when you allow yourself to immerse within that flow.

Stop struggling; allow your Collective to guide you, as they are guided by their Guardians and Mentors. What is your purpose? To Remember you've already graduated. Your personality within the framework of earth must be reeducated, but your spirit has easy access to your inner Collective to help make the personality education easier.

Now to get on with your purpose. Once you are educated and in line with your Collective (or your spirit guides as some of you call them), they will guide you, but you must listen! Learn to pay attention to the subtle messages all around you. Collectively the number of graduates on the earth is tremendous. Collectively you must work together to help the children. From the most basic needs to their spiritual development. And this must be done before they reach the age of puberty.

What can you do? It is the question you should all be asking yourselves. Let that be your mantra. What should I be doing to help the children? It can be within your community, a neighborhood, your own children, or working with global organizations. Your Inner Collective will guide you.

Then when these children reach a more mature age, create opportunities for them to express their creativity for what they would like to see done in the world. They are tremendous teachers. Begin Youth Councils for leadership. Not as YOU would like to see, but how THEY would like it. Each child has a tremendous storehouse of inner wisdom and knowledge available that gets educated out as they grow older, unless they are nurtured to be creatively FREE and taught Inner Listening Skills.

As they grow into adulthood they will then have confidence in their Inner Listening Skills to know what their purpose is. Wouldn't you all have liked to grown up fully conscious and connected with your inner Collective? To know that each of you had this? Teach your children about their inner Collective.

If time and energy are spent on the children, then the Lightworkers' work would be done and they would not have to Awaken All on the Earth who are Ignorant for there would not be any left. We are in transition times now to do both kinds of work. Awaken the Ignorant and prepare the children so they never go to sleep.

They must also be taught about the Five Minds. Ellie, we were instrumental in sending you the information about the Five Minds. Teach this so that the inner Collective voice is not confused with the personality minds.

E: Yes, I will do this. (*See Addendum.*)

Homer: There are threads of Tone and Light coming together that are in harmony and nearly ready to be sent about training programs for the children. They are to be used by the Lightworkers as they work with children. Many of you can tap into these streams of Tone and Light. Know that these streams are available.

Use your own Inner Listen Skills. Use the Five Principles of Inner Listening: *Desire* it above all else, *Know* it is possible, *Discipline* yourselves to do the work of *Contemplation* with a sense of *Wonder*. Use these tools to access this information.

Do you think it is easy for our friend here to be sitting down nearly everyday doing this work? It is not. We have made it physically uncomfortable for her NOT to do it because it was her agreement (not consciously) but it was her agreement to do this work. She can speak more to you of this if she chooses.

Only those of you willing to use the Five Principles to Inner Contact will achieve what you wish to know. When you do (IF you do) the rewards are tremendous for you will begin to fully awaken into your purpose.

95

That is all for today on this.

Addenda

Note from Ellie

In a paragraph before, "That is all for today on this" I received personal information about Rainbow Sun Qigong that I edited to another page thinking it not appropriate for this book. However, the people who received the original transcripts have strongly requested me not to take anything out, so here is what was said:

Homer: Now about Rainbow Sun Qigong. Ellie these are personal messages for you in the development of this form. The first video project is targeted for seniors and adults but the purpose is for the children.

For the seniors it is for each to remember their healthy, youthful body. Have them picture themselves when at their most healthy and vital with clear eye sight, healthy heart, lungs and digestion, strong muscles and bones. Through the Rainbow Sun they absorb all that is healthy.

Have them visualize themselves when they were at their optimum health while keeping the wisdom from their life experiences. That is the visualization for them to use with the Rainbow Sun meditation.

Have them breathe into each organ - using their minds - Strength, Vitality and Appreciation for all their life experiences. Direct them to ask Rainbow Sun, "What one thing can I do for myself today to revitalize my body, mind or spirit." Make sure to remind them to listen for the answer and take appropriate action. This will help people tremendously.

The Five Minds

The Five Minds is a concept I developed (or thought I developed!) as a way to explain how different aspects of ourselves had its own agenda without regard to the others. They are the First or Physical Mind, the Second or Emotional Mind, the Third or Intellectual Mind, the Fourth or Spirit Mind and the Fifth Mind.

Briefly, the Physical Mind is located in the lower belly area called *dan tien* (from my Qigong training and pronounced don tee en). You might call it the second Chakra. (I don't work with the Chakra system as this has never made sense to me and has not resonated with my personal energy experiences with the body; whereas the Chinese energy model has been in line with my own experiences.) The Physical Mind has an agenda that deals only with its physical wants, needs and desires regardless of consequences or rational thinking. It has no need to be loved - only food, shelter and sex - not always in that order. Also, physical health and the desire to have things that will enhance the physical experience.

The Second Mind, the Emotional Mind, resides in the solar plexus area, called the Golden Bowl in my Qigong training. It is where our emotional vulnerability and history reside. The Emotional Mind has one agenda; to be cared about, often times confused with being loved.

In its unhealthy form it is confused with love and completely conditional, such as, "I'll love you if . . . " or "If you loved me you'd . . . . " It can be very immature and childlike if the terms 'caring' and 'loving' are confused. For the most part, the Emotional Mind can only be satisfied if it feels loved according to how it has defined what love is.

97

Sometimes people think this resides in the heart, but upon further meditation on this I know it to reside within the solar plexus. Emotional love is not from the heart. It is from a gut feel and primal need to be cared about which is the mature form of the Second Mind. Everyone needs to be cared about to be emotionally healthy.

The Third Mind, or Intellectual Mind, resides in the back of the head regulating reason and logic. Its agenda is to gather information and "always be right." It doesn't care about being fed or loved. It only wants to be fed information. It tends to be arrogant, detached and thinks it is superior, or above, the lower two minds.

This Mind tries to make rational sense of life experiences so it can grow and learn. It doesn't like to be embarrassed, so it works hard to learn quickly so as not to make the same mistake twice; however, it is not always successful.

The Fourth Mind, or Spirit Mind, (I have specifically not called it the Spiritual Mind because there are too many connotations with the word "Spiritual") resides in the center and front part of the head called upper *dan tien*. Its doesn't have an agenda, but a purpose to make the connection between the spirit and the physical realms. It regulates intuition. It is a gentler mind and needs to be invited in to participate.

It will leave whenever there is aggression from any of the lower three minds because it has no agenda to play any of the lower mind games. However, the Fourth Mind can be the greatest source of strength in times of crisis if it is fully cultivated and utilized.

It expresses in many subtle ways, such as feelings within the body or knowing something without reason. It is most often known as the "still small voice." It is the most powerful mind

98

we have and is typically the least developed, and the le
To the general public it is also the least understood of
Minds.

The Fifth Mind can be activated only if one is cognisant
of how the Fourth Mind works and actively working with the
Fourth Mind. It resides in the heart or middle *dan tien*, and is
expressed as unconditional love. It recognizes love as an action
and not a feeling. It thinks globally rather than locally, although
local action can and will be taken if it is in line with global
thinking. It cannot be contained and is expressed as free spirited
or eccentric. Its action can seem ruthless if it is on a mission of
a higher purpose since it has little patience with the antics of the
lower minds.

The Fifth Mind works in full partnership with the Fourth
Mind, consciously working with the Spirit Realm to take action
in the physical realm if it is appropriate. You might feel it as one
who has love expressed as power, and feel it as if that person
is "a force of nature." Power, without any thought to abuse
power, but power to be used as a vehicle or catalyst for positive
change.

One who lives by the Fifth Mind may seem detached and
unfeeling, when, in fact, they embody the purest love. The Fifth
Mind is not manipulated by any of the lower three minds, but
uses them to sever its higher purpose.

There are three *dan tiens* that correspond to three of the five
minds. The lower belly area called the lower *dan tien* (First
Mind), the heart center called the middle *dan tien* (Fifth Mind),
and the third eye area called the upper *dan tien* (Fourth Mind).
These have also been called the Three Treasures, or *jing* (vitality,
lower), *qi* (energy, middle) and shen (spirit, upper). The literal
translation of *dan tien* is "Sea of Energy."

99

17

Spirit Historian

12 May 2003

Centering. Open.

Voice: Dear One, you are learning well now how to let go so it makes the contact easier.

E: Where is Homer?

Voice: He is with Marge today.

E: Who are you? You don't feel like my Collective.

Voice: (Ignoring me and continuing as if I never asked a question) In ancient times upon the earth, the native people lived. They were not conscious, only animals. Many died. The earth was harsh. These beings were created out of the thought/sound/light patterns of the Creative Force. What is created, however, must be looked after, and so it was agreed to join these creations of ours into Collectives.

We became the Guardians of the Collectives while they matured. We would send them thought streams to initiate an impulse within their mind for ways to make their life easier. We activated the brain tissue to develop and it became a receptor to our messages. There was easy communication between us. As they developed they began independent thought and decision making. We encouraged this so we could give up our Guardianship over our creation, but without us their lives

101

reverted back to chaos. By this time many lost contact with us and the ability to communicate directly.

We directed those who could still communicate, and they became leaders over the Unconscious Ones. Those who continued their contact grew and developed into higher levels of being while others still lived and acted like animals. Creation itself is pulsing tones going out in waves. It is easy to create. It is not so easy to bring a creation into consciousness. For this requires higher levels of thought. Even thought alone will not make one conscious. Many think but are brutal, animalistic. This is not consciousness.

Consciousness can come only when the Spark of The One is activated. The Spark is a Light/Tone imbedded into a creation, and it is this Spark that renders consciousness when activated . The Spark can be dormant within a creation indefinitely until there is a strong desire for that creation to KNOW something more - to have contact with its creator. 'Is there not more? Is this all there is?' That is when the Spark of The One is activated and consciousness begins - true consciousness.

This is why we continue to say the children must be awakened. Do all you can to awaken this Spark within the children so they live their lives in an awakened state. It is the KEY to bringing Peace on Earth. It is the Key to your freedom; it is the Key to OUR freedom from continued Guardianship. For once the Spark of The One is awakened, there can be direct contact with the Light and Sound of The One. There can be no child left wanting to know it is loved and that it is special. No child. NO CHILD, no matter the age. This is the message we wish to impart. Teach the children; awaken their Spark.

E: How is this best done?

Voice: Each Lightworker has gone back with, or developed, a set of skills necessary to do his/her part. It is essential for each one to determine how best to use these skills and to be guided in partnership with their Collective. Some do not want to work directly with children but have gone back to work with the Lost Ones, the ones that have grown up in ignorance. Honor your teachers above all else. They are the true Lightworkers on the planet - the teachers of the children and those teachers who work with the Lost Ones.

Addenda

Note from Ellie

To honor the requests of not taking anything out, I will put back the personal message I received about Rainbow Sun Qigong. The Voice continued . . .

Voice: We will begin a training for teaching people how to awaken the Spark within the children and others. It will be very simple. The Rainbow Sun Meditation we sent you is part of it, for within the Rainbow Sun Meditation we have embedded Tones within the colors that will awaken all who do this meditation. They must simply be open and receptive to hearing the Tones within.

E: Could you give more information now?

Voice: Begin with silence and moving within, along with the movements as we have shown you in Rainbow Sun Qigong. Visualize the Rainbow Sun. The training is the Rainbow Sun Qigong! That is all you need. It is all within the form. It is a simple form, but we will use it to activate the Spark of The One using this. Children will understand it easily.

Interruption from my kids.

4 months later

We completed the Rainbow Sun Qigong video project for Seniors and I presented it to the National Qigong Association Annual Conference in Asheville, NC in August 2003. We were so far behind schedule on it (because of all the time Homer's entrance into my life was taking) we had to ship duplication equipment to Atlanta, where we stayed for a couple of days before the conference. We were duplicating throughout the conference behind a baby grand piano to keep up with the sales.

Experienced Qigong practitioners loved the form and we nearly sold out of videos. Many schoolteachers at the conference attended the workshop, knowing our next video project was Qigong for Kids using Rainbow Sun Qigong. Someone even volunteered to field-test it for us in the classroom. It appears that Rainbow Sun is going out into the world. And I'm being shown, step by step through example, how these inner partnerships work.

An amazing "coincidence" happened when filming Rainbow Sun Qigong for Seniors; on the exact two days we were going to film my mother (71) and grandmother (92) "happened" to be in Tucson . . . . from Minnesota. Their beautiful presence in the video added so much. Was this the Spirit Realm helping again? This coincidence makes me wonder if the Spirit Realm wanted to make their presence/participation so obvious I couldn't possibly miss it.

104

18

Blue Light Tunnel Meditation

13 May 2003

Note from Ellie: Today a friend of mine called, wondering if Homer or my Collective had anything that might help her since she is dealing with a health-related situation. I looked at this as an experiment to see what would happen. Working through the opening of Homer and my Collective, we were successful in making contact with her Collective, who then guided us on how to proceed.

It was interesting to access someone else's Collective. This may be a point of interest for those researching this kind of communication. For now I will center and go in to see if there are any messages for the group tomorrow night *(See Addendum)*, or whatever comes in. Centering. Open.

Collective: We are celebrating. You are now in the world but not of the world. Doing this work in direct communication with your inner Collective yields a fuller life and a living of life as we have foreseen all to do. Continue to be guided by this flow. Now Homer would like to speak to the metaphysical group.

Homer: Hi, Marge, Marcia and the rest. It is good to see you and your support of this kind of work. Groups like this are very important holders of Light and Sound, no matter your personal awakening (spiritual maturity). Marcia, you just finished Mystery School. You are still unfolding what you learned there. I have been in contact with your Collective and others who lead that Mystery School. There is great work going on, but the most important work is for all of you to begin conscious contact with your inner Councils.

There is much work to do in the world and within the dimensions you function in. It is all quite exciting, and I wish I had words to describe the fullness of life you are living, besides the small part you are allowed to remember, while an aspect of yourself is on the earth. Know there is so much more you are doing at all times.

The reason to get into full conscious contact with your Council is so to know your purpose and fulfill it. Your Council will direct you into remembering step-by-step. It may not be easy. You will have to trust and question anything that doesn't seem right - that is good, too. Discernment on your part will keep the communication clear. Use discernment but keep your sense of Wonder.

'How, Homer, how?' I'm always hearing this from you. *(Homer is not addressing me, he is addressing those reading this.)* Stop asking me this! Stop thinking I have all the answers! Just because I'm on this side and have a fuller understanding of our fuller life doesn't mean I have all the answers. If you have a question then I have to go seek out someone who might have the answer. Why not learn the skills yourself to access your Council and work with them to help you get the answers? Your Council is made up of a bunch of Homers! But they are your Council, there specifically for YOU.

Sit quietly now as I guide you into a meditation to contact your Council. For this contact remember you must Desire the contact above all else, Know it is possible, and be open with a sense of Wonder.

Close your eyes and bring your attention to your chest.

106

Breathe into your chest, letting all tension go with the out breath. Picture yourself standing at the opening of an arched tunnel. Begin to walk into the tunnel. The tunnel is filled with beautiful pieces of art work, and you hear beautiful strands of music. Continue to walk further into the tunnel.

Now you see Light at the other end. You get excited. The Light and Music get stronger as you walk down the tunnel. You begin to see glimpses of grass, a water source, park benches as you look out. Children playing and flying kites. As you get closer to the end of the tunnel, ready to walk out onto the grass, you see the blue sky. Large trees surround the park. Many people are milling around.

Within this park is your Council. They are waiting for you. Let your feet guide you to any area of the park you wish to go. Enjoy wherever you find yourself in the park. Now open your thoughts to making contact with your full Council. To do this, close your eyes (within this visualization). Take a nice deep breath in; when you exhale, open your eyes and your Council will be surrounding you while in the park. Do this now. We will sit in silence while you communicate with your Council.

Remember not to hold on too tightly to expectation or you will lose the contact. Stay in the flow . . . . detached. Ask what messages they have for you or have them answer any questions you might have.

When you are finished, thank them. You can go back through this tunnel to the park at any time you wish to meet your Council, but now it is time to go. Walk back to the tunnel exit and enter it. Walk back to the tunnel entrance passing all the artwork and hearing the music fade. Come out of the tunnel, back to your body here in this room. Open your eyes. Please share your experiences.

Homer: There is a Higher One who wishes to speak to you now.

Higher One: We have sent you this meditation through Homer to develop your Inner Listening Skills for contact with your Collective. Your Collective is your entry way into the Higher Realms. Your Collective will allow you to access information when appropriate. You may also communicate with your Collective's Guardians. Your Collective can bring in experts for you when needed.

It is a very rich way to live your life. Be 'in the world but not of the world.' This type of communication is the way to do this. It does not mean you are to be involved only with things of a spiritual nature; it does not mean to live your life with only physical concerns. It means to live with both in balance. Then LIVE, Learn and Share. That is all.

Addenda

Note from Ellie

I was going to give a presentation the following night to a metaphysical group in Tucson who knew Homer and Marge; they had presented dowsing to this same group. By now many of these people had heard Homer was communicating through me and were looking forward to hearing the story first hand, rather than the presentation I had originally prepared. This was going to be my first public presentation about Homer.

I was scared. Marge called to say she'd sit by me and hold my hand; Homer showed up before the presentation started. Marge in the physical and Homer in the spiritual, standing by me, so I could share their story. Wow! In a million years I never could have seen myself doing this. Marcia, the woman who originally invited me to speak to their group, knew Homer and Marge. This is whom Homer is referring to when he begins to speak.

4 months later

The meditation that came through was eventually called the Blue Light Tunnel Meditation later in the writings because of all the Blue Light streaming in the tunnel. I have found the more I share the meditation and the more people use it, the more distinct the tunnel is becoming. The floor of the tunnel had originally been concrete, and now it's a path of golden light.

As I'm writing this Homer showed up and is saying, "connect the dots . . ." (It took me a moment, but I get what he wants me to convey.) In Chapter 13, four days prior to this writing, the first hints of this meditation came through. I have copied it below to show . . . . . . Oh, Homer wants to say it. One moment while I go in . . .

Homer: Information will sometimes come through very clearly, other times the mind pathways are clogged and so the information will come trickling in. This was an intentional thing we have done to demonstrate the importance of regular inner contact with your Council. The more contact you have the easier the communication. It is spiritual exercise, like physical exercise, pumping the channels clear rather than pumping the muscles!

E: I keep hearing "regular inner contact" repeated with emphasis over and over again . . .

Here is what was said in Chapter 13.

E: I know others will want to know how to contact their own Collectives . . . . .

I see discussion within the group occurring . . . . . no words, but a picture/visual. I'll do my best here. It looks like entering through an arch of a really big underground overpass into a garden/park with many milling about.

E: Can people access their collective through this visualization?

Collective: Yes, one way is to visualize walking through a tunnel to a park with intention to meet their Collective. It is for the individual to go to the beings who *feel* familiar.

19

Ascension

14 May 2003

Note from Ellie: I awoke early this morning and started to feel the familiar "buzz" of Homer. It was stronger today than it has been. Also, Marge gave me a 1995 article about Suzy Smith and her research experiment about life after death. (Suzy worked with Dr. Gary Schwartz at the Human Energy Systems Laboratory at the University of Arizona researching the after life.) According to the article before Suzy crossed over she came up with some kind of code that can be unlocked from a common saying or piece of poetry or a bit of nursery rhyme. The code is hidden in a Florida bank vault.

Mostly I don't think about it, but since I read the article I keep hearing "Peter Piper picked a peck of pickled peppers." I don't know what the context is; I just keep hearing it in my head. All I know is when I read the article I knew it wasn't a common saying or piece of poetry; I get a very strong feeling it is a nursery rhyme.

Then last night, out of the blue, I was hearing Harry Chapin lyrics in my head over and over again and had a feeling it was connected to the article, "The cat's in the cradle with a silver spoon, little boy blue and the man in the moon." Who knows if this means anything or if it is Suzy. My guess is not - I didn't know her or anything about her, but since I'm documenting things I thought I'd write this, too.

I feel a very strong buzz. Interruption. A morning dove

was looking at me from by the pond out my office window. It was acting distressed, looking at me, then at the pond, when I noticed a wing flapping at the edge of the pond. I ran outside to get the bird out, but it was too late. It was a quail, still warm in my hand. I'm sad to hear others in its flock calling. What is this about? Yesterday I found a dead lizard. And what's with the dove looking at me as if it thinks I can understand it?

Centering. Open.

Homer: Resurrection. Ascending.

E: I feel myself experiencing a lifting up out of my body . . . I'm feeling light headed.

Homer: Today the topic is Ascension. It has been a topic within the New Age community for some time. Ascension is a lifting up of the Spirit to gain access to spiritual information in the Higher Realms. When the Spirit is able to lift itself up and out of the consciousness it currently has, it is able to access other realms of information. For example, if a preschooler wanted to access information at a medical school library, he/she couldn't. He/she wouldn't have the skills or maturity necessary to do so. It takes training and a step-by-step progression, personal discipline, drive, desire and interest in the field to achieve this.

With Ascension it is the same. You need the skills and maturity necessary to ascend into the Higher Realms to access Spiritual Information. The Final Ascension from earth is a return of the small strand of consciousness back to its whole. Some call it returning Home - like a family member out on travel returning home.

E: What is the purpose of going to earth?

112

Homer: Creation. Experimentation. Awakening others there who are not yet conscious. Teaching. Liberation. There are many reasons to go to earth. Each person must do his/her own work. And it is work. And it takes a strong desire to do so. Not everyone has this strong desire. They can learn from others just as a student can learn from its teachers. A student can build on the knowledge of the teacher but must experience it alone to forge new ground of understanding.

In matters of Spirit it must be experienced first-hand. Inner Listening Skills are necessary to do this. The mind of an earthling is so strong it can easily drown the Inner Voice. It is a subtle voice, but once you are attuned to it, it is very loud. You will hear the voice in all things - in the waterfalls, in the drowning of a bird. The voice is loud because it is reflected in ALL things. It is like breaking a secret code. Once you have the information necessary to break the code, a code is no longer encoded. Or like those three dimensional pictures. You look at the picture and don't see anything until an image pops out at you. But you must be trained to see the picture.

Often times, no *always*, all your messages are right in front of you but you don't see them because you are not trained to see them. The Native American people could look at a rock or stream and know things. They were great listeners. This Inner Listening must be taught again. You must teach yourselves to pay more attention.

Ask your Council, 'What would you have me see today? Who would you have me speak to today? What are you trying to show me or teach me today?' Then pay attention. It might be a song, a poem, a child saying something. Pay attention. Learn the language of the Spirits. It is your language. Open your Inner

113

Eye to see. Open your Inner Ear to hear. Open your Inner Heart to feel.

It is Mind that gets in the way, that tries to trick you. The Mind can act like an Inner Voice, but it is the trickster leading you away from your inner seeing and hearing. You must stay focused on what you wish to hear and see.

If you have animals, listen to them. You know what I'm talking about. They communicate to you in subtle ways. It is more than action-reward-training. There is also communication occurring. Your plants will speak to you. Listen. Listen. Listen. It is all around you.

Ask your Inner Council to help you. Then Listen. Your life is much fuller with this Inner Listening. Dowsers learn to listen using the physical tools of the rods or pendulum. These are tools of Inner Listening, but soon you will not even need the tools. You will sense more easily by the subtle feeling you receive in your body. The Inner Listening instinct will become strong again. It is a subtle instinct but very strong once developed.

Sometimes you ignore things and then afterwards say, 'I knew that. I don't know how, but I knew that. I don't know why I didn't pay more attention.' Paying attention can save you much heartache. Learn to listen. Even then you might miss the signals, but it is for you to keep trying. And you may take a lifetime or more to learn. It is always for you to learn to listen in more and more subtle ways.

Begin by journaling. Journaling is one of the greatest tools you have. You don't have to know what you will write about, but begin a regular habit of speaking with your Inner Council. You will feel as if you are making it up. That is a good start. Just keep doing it. It will reveal wonderful messages for you. Another thing to learn is your astrological influences and the

Tarot. These are tools to help you learn to distinguish the subtle messages. These are all external tools - tools that help develop the subtle Inner Listening. Dowsing, journaling, Tarot, astrological influences. These things will all help you.

Now we will begin to outline an Inner Listening Skill Course so you may master Ascension into the Higher Realms for your spiritual information.

Begin with a six-month course - a weekly program. Begin with an Introduction class. Have each person apply for the program by submitting a ten-page essay on why he or she wants to be part of the program and what they have already done in their spiritual development. Okay, a three- to five-page essay is good.

Not everyone will be accepted into the program. Some must first learn other lessons. It will not need to be decided by the teacher. These students will automatically be eliminated by life experience and when a better time for them comes, they will know it. Most who are attracted to the program will have been doing this work already but will want to have a group to play with.

Once a group is gathered, blend the energies of the group. Have them do circling dances with their eyes closed. Breathing exercises with each other. Hand exercises with each other. Qigong and Shamanic journeying. Journaling. Have a time of discussion.

Each class will be two hours. The first 30 minutes will be discussion of what was found in journaling and other weekly assignments. The second 30 minutes will be teaching time through physical or energetic exercises. The third 30 minutes will be Shamanic Journeying with Journaling. The last 30 minutes will be sharing, with new assignments given out. The mission and purpose of this course will be to focus each person in developing his/her Inner Listening Skills.

There will be no answers from the facilitator, but mentoring and guidance into looking higher for the answers. Each student will be allowed to discuss matters with others in the class. All will learn to go within for answers and share how they did so and what answers they received. It will be a step-by-step mentoring process into Inner Listening.

20

"The Work"

23 May 2003

Note from Ellie: I have been in Minneapolis for the past week. There were three days when I felt the buzzing, indicating it would be a good time to sit down to write, but I was busy and ignored it. As a result I experienced many dizzy spells and the top of my head hurt more than usual.

My last day there I began to develop a headache - I now call them my psychic headaches. By the time I went to dinner with a friend at 6:00 p.m., I had to ask for an aspirin. It didn't put even a dent in it; the top of my head felt as if it were going to blow off it hurt so bad.

At one point during dinner, I heard a voice say, "Give Kathi a reading." I ignored it, and not ninety seconds later Kathi said, "You know, maybe you should give me a reading." I laughed at the idea of me trying to control the communication as I felt myself falling inward and giving her a reading.

Afterwards, I was totally clear; my body didn't hurt, my headache was completely gone, and my head didn't feel fuzzy any longer. Giving the reading was like blowing my pipes clean; resisting the communication gives me a lot of pain. I got back to Tucson yesterday and took today to rest because I was exhausted, but all day I kept hearing whispering in my ears, "Tomorrow you will write?" I finally acknowledged I would, so here I am.

Centering. Opening. Feeling dizzy. Feeling the "Homer

buzz."

Homer: Your observation is correct. Your headaches come from resistance. Stay with the flow and all will be well.

E: What is so important that I need to be the 'phone line' for you to communicate?

Homer: It is not for you and me. We are only servants who do work for the Higher Ones. They direct it all. For myself, I have gotten the hang of things here now. It is not what I expected. I'm beginning to be able to move into more dimensions, but this stream of consciousness stays here. I'm beginning to awaken to my whole self - WHOLE SELF. The stream of consciousness that speaks to you as Homer, and holds this communication open, is a small part of the whole. A very small part. It is no wonder I cannot describe it all to you in words. For now I will pass on what the Higher Ones wish and what will be helpful for those living on earth.

Purpose & Mission

E: I feel the "Homer buzz" leave and a shifting within . . .

Other Voice: Remember who you are. You are all Great Ones who have locked yourselves away in the distractions of the earth. You are there to do The Work. Each and everyone of you reading this has a purpose and mission. 'What is my mission?' we hear you ask. You must discover this through Inner Dialog with your Collective, for each Collective has a mission and purpose of which you are a part.

For some it may be to sing or dance or do art work and bring through the beauty you only half remember. Art is to be that of

118

beauty. Ugliness is only that of the earth, that of suffering aᵢ pain. Ugliness is not art work; it is a representation of non-remembering and the suffering that happens as a result.

So remember! Remember, then create out of love and song and beauty; hope and faith and trust; knowing, synergy and flow. When art work comes from these things, it is from the Inner Dimensions. If it is not of these things it comes from the unawakened mind feeling lost and in pain. All art and music are to rejoice and be in celebration, for that awakens remembering within all who see or hear it. Art and music is for awakening.

A Doctor Speaks About Healing & Health

E: Silence. . . . . as if a phone is being handed to someone else.

Voice: Hello? Hello?

E: Yes?

Voice: Oh, I haven't done this kind of communication before.

E: Who are you?

Male Voice: Robert was my name while on earth, Robert Edwards. I was a doctor. They tell me I am a doctor in many lifetimes. I wish to speak to doctors. Healing comes from an awakening of the spiritual within yourself. When you awaken to the spiritual within yourself you open the channel for direct communication with your Inner Council. You sometimes get a 'feeling' you should do such and such. That is part of your Inner Council. Learn to make direct contact with them.

There are doctors here who would like to help direct your

119

work with you. Your systems of healthcare create
l healthcare. It is for you to remember you are not
...c working on a machine. You are working with
threads of consciousness within a shell or vessel. Focus on the
consciousness, not the shell. That is where true healing will
happen.

Now, for those of you directed to help keep the shell working
properly, your job is nutrition. Nutrition, nutrition, nutrition. I
can't emphasize this enough. Why? Because as the body is
polluted, the mind gets sleepier, and all sense of consciousness
gets lost within the foggy-mind until there is no remembering.
When there is no remembering, there is no hope; when there
is no hope, people do drastic things in order to feel - including
murder and rape and war and thrill-seeking behaviors. Not as a
celebration of life, but to FEEL.

They can't feel because they have lost contact with their
spiritual connection which gives meaning to life. It is like
cutting yourself off from your entire family, then forgetting you
had a family for emotional support. There is no one to say I care
about you. No one to say you are special. No one to praise your
efforts or give you advice. It is all gone. It is lonely and empty.
Healing is healing of the spirit. That is the true doctor.

Nutrition is the way for the medical profession to keep
the shell healthy; then your hospitals would empty out except
for those things from accidents, like broken bones. Nutrition
comes from food, which comes from the land, so the land must
be clean. Your priority is to clean the land. Grow healthy foods
and eat in moderation, only in moderation. This is your work to
do to be a good doctor. Learn more about nutrition. Insist the
medical schools spend a great deal of time on educating doctors
on this. It is essential to people waking up spiritually.

120

If you are not a doctor, it is for you to take your your own hands and educate yourself. Take control and responsibility for doing this. It is important. Those close to starvation are better off than those who gorge themselves into sleepiness. Neither is good, find the middle way and be healthy through good nutrition.

Teach the children. They are the priority so they grow up eating correctly and know the rules of nature. For nature is not forgiving. You abuse the law and the shell will fall. It is a great waste of your resources dealing with nutrition related illness. Do it now. Take responsibility now.

Exercise. The body must move to flush out the toxins or the toxins stagnate within the tissue and grow into cancers. Keep the body moving. Moving. Moving. Keep active. Moving keeps the mind clear. Keep your mind active, also. Educate yourself throughout your life. And pray, however that looks like to you, pray. Keep the Inner Dialog open between you and your Council. That is all.

Homer: Marge, it is time we get out for some walks and get some exercise Walk and I will walk beside you. You have work to do and that shell needs to be healthy to do our work. (*See Addendum.*)

The Blue Light

E: . . . . . Nothing for a while. . . . .

Voice: Blue Light. The Blue Light is where The One dances. It is the Higher Realms. Not as in 'higher away' from you or 'better than' you, but the Higher Realms where The One dances in the Dance of Creation. It is the core of where everyone comes from. All come of the Blue Light. 'Out of the

121

blue,' remember? Out of the blue something came. It comes out of the Creative Impulse. When you are tapped into the Creative Impulse of The One, your life can be transformed

E: How?

Voice: By making this connection means that you will have had to awaken out of the shell's sleepiness into conscious contact - sometimes unconscious contact - with your Inner Collective. By prayer and fasting this contact is made. Through a pure body, mind and spirit this contact is make.

The Work is to refine your Spirit enough to make this contact, and while doing the work to refine your spirit, your life is made better. It is why the first rule for Inner Dialog is Desire it above all else. For then the necessary work may be done to refine your spirit, personality and body. Envelop yourself in the Blue Light and you are in Bliss. In this Blue Light is abundance, joy, fullness, completeness, abundance, health and awareness, and your cellular activation begins.

E: Cellular activation? What is this?

Voice: A cellular activation occurs when you have refined yourselves enough that you can have direct contact with the Higher Ones. Your energy must be adjusted to carry such a frequency. It is not done through some grand ceremony someone comes up with. You cannot even plan it. All you can do is develop inner contact with your Collective, refining your spirit, and the Blue Light will spontaneously happen, and your life will not be the same.

It is a matter of Desiring it above all else without COVETING it, for that will get you nowhere. Knowing it is

122

possible without WANTING it. It is different.

We reiterate to you the Five Keys to Inner Dialog: Desire, Knowing, Discipline, Contemplation, Wonder. These are important for you to remember, for when you are weary and don't remember where you are, come back to these and see what you have forgotten. It will keep you on track. That is all for today.

Addendum

4 months later

When I was originally editing the transmission for spelling errors, I almost took the part out about Homer and Marge getting out for a walk. I had no idea what their lifestyle had been and my ego didn't want to leave it in and get "caught" for being a fraud. I was already feeling like one with some of the things coming through.

It wasn't until I received Marge's introduction for this book, four days before going to print, that I read how meaningful that little walking message was to her. Or that it was confirmation for her it really was Homer speaking. This made me feel like maybe there was something to this writing.

21

The Three Fastings

24 May 2003

Centering, Opening. The "Homer buzz" begins right away.

Homer: I wish everyone to know I am well. More than well. For I have more freedom here than many. Why? Because I learned to free my mind when I was living on the earth. There are so many here who limit their experience according to their thinking and beliefs. Oh, to say it is all an illusion is so true. There are many helpers on this side, just as there are on your side, and we all work to awaken the sleeping masses.

We are able to do so much more than we have thought. Jesus said we will do what he did and more. MORE! I say and He says. Do not put yourselves below the Great Teacher, but believe in him to show you what you are capable of. Yes, you. David. And Sue, and Mary, and Theresa, and Bob, and on and on and on to name ALL people of the earth. You all have magic within you, the magic of the Great Laws, which govern Creation. To achieve these things requires prayer and fasting. There is someone here who wishes to speak on this.

Other Voice: Today I wish to speak on the true nature of Fasting. It is a fasting of what you know within your heart to be holding you back - a giving up of what you *know* holds you back. For that knowing is a spiritual impulse within you. There are Three Fastings.

The First Fasting is physical. How can you hear if you are

125

cted by the sleepy mind, which comes from what you put ur body and a lack of activity? Learn what is natural in food and drink and movement. If you do not know, learn from someone who does.

If you overeat, learn moderation; that is your Fast. This is not to say to starve yourself, for that is much too easy and is a distraction from the real work, but to learn moderation and give up those things holding sway over you. Fasting without food and water is not a good thing for most people and will bring harm.

If you do not engage in movement and deep breathing, then your Fast is to give up that lack. Moving the body to activate deep breathing, and eating in moderation that which is natural, will sustain you so your body has nourishment, yet your mind remains free from the sleepiness that foods and lack of activity create. You are not to be guilt-ridden over this; that too is a distraction of the mind - but to hear the Spiritual Call for action.

The Second Fasting is of the mind. It is a fasting from thoughts you know within your heart to be holding you back. Eliminate the activities and relationships engaged in for escape and distraction. Listen to music, read what inspires you, meditate and sit in silence, using visualizations that bring joy to your heart and mind. Heed the Inner Impulses and engage in mental activities that Inspire. Leave all else behind you that is not kind for your mind or others.

The Third Fasting is of the emotions. It is a fasting from extreme negative emotions you feel within, for when you engage in this activity, you enter into the manifesting impulse to create chaos within your life and others. Enter into a fasting period from these emotions until they calm, then do what you

126

can to maintain this state no matter what is happening in your life. When you do this you enter into the Sacred Waters of Inner Listening, even in crisis.

'What is the Spiritual Call,' I hear you ask? It is when you receive an Impulse from within for Spiritual Renewal, Growth or Action. It is not something easily heard if you are in the midst of great activity - but when you create openings for silence, you will feel it and know it more strongly as you cultivate the Three Fastings.

I hear your cry, 'How do I hear the Inner Impulses? How do I know I am doing the right thing?' Follow the Middle-Way, where there are no extremes within the body, the mind or the emotions. With this training you will but flow into what is natural. The negative habits of body, mind and emotions hold you back from contact with Inner Listening. Learn to cultivate the Three Fastings, for then you will have all you need for Inner Listening to happen naturally.

Life is for you to live. You can live it however you wish, but why not live it in fullness? It will serve you in that life and in your life on this side.

A Guardian Speaks: No Excuses!

Another Voice: For now, create daily contemplation time. Do not speak to me or complain to me that you have no time. You do not have time to do otherwise or you get lost in the illusions of earth. I am one of the Guardians of the Collectives and the greatest number of thought-streams we hear is a pitying, sorry-for-self, depression.

Do you not see that this too is part of the illusion. Step away from it and make a choice. Make a choice to enhance your Spirit. It takes work and discipline to do this. It is not for the faint-hearted. It is the job of the Spiritual Warrior. It is the work you must do to war within yourself.

When you have the conviction that this is what you wish, you will be tested over and over to go back to your old ways. This is the natural way, the law, to test your Desire. You will be tested, but your purpose is to stay on the path.

How? By staying inspired and eliminating all that is negative from your life. Have a daily diet of what is positive. I repeat, have a daily diet of what is positive, be it music, song, word or deed; movies, art, children, or laughter; flowers, hiking, nature or water. Have a daily diet of what nurtures YOU. You must have this.

If you are unable to get out of bed, imagine it. Imagine it so hard that you can smell the roses, you can hear the music. Desire your inner freedom above all else. It will free you. Then you will more easily hear the Inner Voices of guidance.

Three Vision Perspectives

Yes, I hear you asking, 'How will I know the voice?' The voice will be all around you in a multitude of ways. Do not worry; you cannot miss it if you know how to read the signs. Learn to look at life from three perspectives.

There is the Land-Walker perspective. You see and name only that which is in front of you in the physical. There is the Water-Way. Are you flowing with ease, holding on or swimming against the current? There is Eagle Vision where you see many sides to a situation and the higher purpose of your lessons, even the painful ones. When you learn to cultivate the Eagle Vision and the Water-Way you will begin to learn the lessons of Inner Listening that cannot be done as a Land-Walker.

you will see meaning in everything. You will begin to

see the ebb and flow of your life and all that is around you. You will begin to be in harmony with nature and its rhythms. You will begin to hear nature sing; you will hear the celestial music that heals all things.

You will hear My Voice in your play, in your lovemaking, in your sadness, in your slumber, in your joy, in your grief, in your death. It is all an ebb and flow of nature; of the Creative Impulse of Shiva, Vishnu and Brahma; of Yin and Yang. Do not resist the flow; learn the flow well.

We have spoken to you before of the usefulness of Astrology and such things as Tarot cards. These are not sacred things; they are practical things. For if you learn to study them, you will begin to see the patterns in your life. Do not take them from the perspective of the Land-Walker, but first from the perspective of the Water-Way. What is the general flow? When does the theme of the cards or stars change? Then over time, look at it from Eagle Vision. What are the over-all themes of your life?

Land-Walker Vision is for immediate observation. Water-Way Vision is for how you are flowing within the immediate situation and on your life-path. Eagle Vision is for the over all patterns in your life. If you view life only from the perspective of the Land-Walker, it will feel bleak, harsh, meaningless, cruel, reactive. Learn the Water-Way and Eagle Vision and your life will be meaningful, spiritual, filled with joy and gladness. That is all for today.

22

Is Homer Leaving?

25 May 2003

Note from Ellie: I'm finding myself with a lot of doubt today. What if I'm making all this up? There seems to be a fine line between inner conversation and my words. I have doubts about continuing this. Maybe not for doing this for myself as a way for me to become clear, but about sharing it.

If I don't share it, then I don't have to feel as if I might be a failure or mislead others. It is easier not to share it. Then there are times that things come through that seem selfish not to share. But how does Homer fit into all this yet? Is it even Homer, or is it my subconscious?

I think I'm also a bit scared today because I'm going to Marge's house and while the people there are explorers and haven't judged me - even made me feel welcomed by their warmth of caring - I feel like it could happen at any minute, which makes me feel vulnerable, which makes me want to hide and not do this. And at the same time I'm getting the buzzy-shaky feeling inside that I'm starting to recognize as plugging into the energy. Why me? Why couldn't this be someone else?

Centering. Opening. "Buzz."

Voice: *(with hand on the back of my head in a comforting way)* Child, it is your destiny to do this work. You are the voice of the Spiritual Realm. 'One Who Speaks for the Spirits.' This is who you are.

131

E: Then what is it you wish to say today?

. . . . . I feel a swelling as if a great wave in the ocean is still cresting . . . . .

The Great Awakening

Voice: The Great Awakening is for the individual and not for the masses. I repeat. The Great Awakening is for the individual and not for the masses! It is an illusion to think otherwise. One step at a time, the seekers tread upon the path, climbing the mountain to their own Great Awakening. It is for the individual. Seek within for direction and study.

Some of you will travel to the East and Middle East. Some will not travel to anywhere. It is not in the where; it is in the how, using the Five Keys to Inner Dialog: Desire, Knowing, Discipline, Contemplation and Wonder. The Inner Dialog will provide the direction.

Do not try too hard, for in grasping it, you lose it. Desire it without holding on too tightly. Desire to stay in the flow. Flow with your awakening. There are many levels to awakening. When you think you have arrived, know you have arrived only at one peak. From there you see many other peaks yet to ascend to. Each is important. Each is always there for the seeker of truth.

Remembering

E: I'm seeing red-cowled figures sitting in meditation . . . . . the whole scene is red . . . . . I'm feeling pressure in the front part of my head . . . . . now the third eye area. This is usually when the Higher Ones come to speak. I ask, 'Is there more for today?'

Voice: Despair is a sickness of the soul where there is no hope.

E: I'm told by many that they do not have the contact I have. I cannot imagine not having this contact. I was willing to die to have it. (*This experience happened in 1978 when I was 18 years old. See Addendum.*)

Voice: Yes, you were willing to die for it. You committed to die for it. Your Desire was so great, and your Despair so great, you refused to eat or drink for three days. Do you remember when we first descended upon you to awaken your centers?

You experienced Grace that night. It is this same Desire, above all things, you must have to awaken. 'Desire above all things' looks differently to you now, does it not? Do you remember? It takes a difficult path to achieve what you have done, and this is not a path for all to take.

E: What happened to me that night?

Voice: What you desired could come only through prayer and fasting, humility and unconditional surrender. You had been on a Spiritual Fast. That is to say, not consciously, but as a flowing out of your consciousness in that moment. You were in despair, and you had a strong-willed determination to KNOW. Does this, too, take on a different meaning for you now? To Know? To know is more than intellectual knowledge. You fundamentally KNEW it was possible, and so you demanded the Inner Contact. Demanded it.

You refused to exist asleep any longer. For that strong Desire, Knowing, Discipline and Contemplation you received Wonder. This is why your are 'One Who Speaks for the Spirits.'

133

This is why. You have chosen not to live any other way, and so you also take up the responsibility of teaching others about what you learn, for many are deaf to direct contact and must receive the information in other ways. That is all. Nothing more. Only what you yourself experience. From that place you have nothing to fear, for if people want the information and it will help them, they will find it. We will direct them to it.

E: . . . . . Once again I'm feeling the waves of pulsing music . . . . like ocean waves coming in . . . . I feel an opening of my heart and belly and whole being . . . . . I bask in these waves pouring through me . . . . . I hear, 'Anything you ask in my name, believing, you shall receive.'

E: I understand now, thank you. I had forgotten and had not made the connection between that long ago period of my life and this happening to me now. I wish to serve. I submit myself once again to service.

. . . . . I continue to feel the waves of pulsing music moving through my body . . . . . My heart feels so open. . . .

Homer Leaves with the Higher Ones
E: Am I to continue working with Marge Hefty and the group she has invited? And please, give me a practical, straight answer. When I feel these beautiful waves pulsing though me, it feels wonderful, but I need the information you send through to be understandable to our experience here and not cryptic.

. . . . . I see Homer now. He is standing in the presence of the Higher Ones, one on each side of him, as if he is going to leave with them. He looks different, not like when I first saw him.

134

He is filled with more light and looks brighter. He feels more detached from the earth work, more impersonal.

E: Why is this?

Higher One: Remember that Homer said he was integrating more and more with his Whole Self. This is what he looks like while in this integration. His 'Homer' stream of consciousness is part of a larger light now. He sends those he loves and cares about waves of this Light and Sound to facilitate their awakening.

E: How is this done? These are nice words and all, but how will Light and Sound help?

Higher One: It washes through the empty spaces and clears. The empty spaces, where thoughts clog up a being. It must be cleared to see the Light and hear the Sound. Homer works to facilitate this for those he cares about.

E: It feels so impersonal.

Higher One: Is the rain impersonal? Yes, but it serves everyone. That is the law. Upon integrating with the Whole Self, the petty concerns of the earth life are washed away. Only the Divine Contact is desired.

E: Is Homer now a part of a Higher One's Collective, yet a stream of his consciousness remains here to help people?

Higher One: Yes, the Whole Self is part of being with a Higher One's Collective. Homer is experiencing now what you have experienced all your life, this connection. Many need to leave that consciousness behind - die a physical death - to experience it.

Homer integrated quickly once here. This was due to prayers he received before he transitioned to this side, his own spiritual work and development on earth, and your association which has caused him to receive the many, many prayers he is receiving still from those who think of him. It is those prayers that are helping to facilitate his integration now.

We feel you struggle with your destiny. You must accept your destiny. You have chosen it. You demanded it; it is not something that can be given back. You cannot go back to sleep. It is time for you to go now. That is all for today.

Addendum

In 1978, when I was 18 years old, I took a semester off from university for a nine-month retreat. I was in spiritual crisis from a decision I made that violated my personal code of ethics. As a result, the severe guilt I experienced from this decision rendered me unable to have any inner dialog. I didn't know how precious it was until I lost it.

It felt as if my life was hollow, bleak and dark black inside. I lost any sense of multidimensionality to my existence; everything appeared flat and lifeless. What had once been a life full of living color, with many layers seen and experienced, had become colorless and dull. I felt as if I were one of the walking dead. I wondered, "How could anyone live like this?" I refused to. I packed my belongings and rented a small apartment in Minnesota I couldn't afford, with no phone and the heat turned off to save money.

One night, shortly after moving in, I made an irrevocable decision. I literally refused to live any longer without God /

Hey You Guys / I didn't care who, talking to me and granting me peace. I couldn't, and wouldn't, live without it for one moment longer.

It was the middle of winter; my apartment was cold. I hadn't been eating much and didn't care. I began to pray - more like cry and yell and scream and demand and curse and cry again. I swore over and over that "they had better talk to me because I wasn't leaving until they did - I didn't care if someone found me dead," and I meant it. I wasn't getting up until I got what I wanted, and I wasn't taking "No" for an answer. For three days I had no sleep, water or food while I pounded an ugly, beat-up reclining chair, praying on my knees, demanding God answer me.

By the third night I was weak and exhausted. The room was freezing. I hadn't eaten or slept; my eyes were swollen from crying; my throat was dry from praying, cursing, yelling and no fluids. The moon was bright, shining through the lead glass windows and I knew I was going to die and didn't care. I had finally given up, surrendered all - even my life.

As I was losing consciousness, I heard music from above me. Celestial music. I looked up. There was no ceiling, only sparkling light. The light was descending down . . . until it reached me, first at my forehead, since I was looking up, then washing down to embrace the whole of my being. As it descended I began to feel warmth and peace flood my body. I was so filled with gratitude, to feel peace and this connection again, all I could do was heave dry sobs.

I fell asleep wrapped in peace on the cold floor with old carpet and nothing but this experience and inner presence. I awoke in the morning toasty warm, as if I'd been wrapped in a fluffy down comforter all night with the heat on. In reality the

137

heat was still turned off and it was the middle of winter, but I didn't notice - I was wrapped in the arms of God.

This experience was the beginning of a much longer soul journey for what occurred in the following months. Seventeen years later I heard a voice say it was time to share what I learned during that mystical nine-month period. I refused to even consider sharing it; it had been a very private experience. But for the next two weeks, day in and day out, during my meditation time, dream time, then into my awake time, I was pestered, "It is time to share what you learned."

I continued to firmly refuse until one day while driving in my car with my two kids in the back seat, I had another mystical experience. I was three blocks from my house when a ball of light whooshed through my body and burst in my chest and belly with the message, "People use the process of manifesting every day of their lives in unconscious ways. It is time NOW for the Healers/Awakened Ones to begin manifesting consciously, to heal themselves, the earth and each other. Go teach this." So . . . . I lost the argument . . . . then made a deal . . . . One day, when the time is right, I'll write that story. In the mean time, I share the information (when I have time) as Conscious Manifesting.

23

Sunday Afternoon at Marge's

26 May 2003

Note from Ellie: Yesterday afternoon I met with Marge and 8 others to explore these writings. We had some discussion about if inner experiences are real or not. One member of the group, Charlie, (whom Homer referenced in the second transmission) said something very insightful to all of us. Something to the effect of, "What difference does it make? If you learn something from it, it doesn't make any difference if it is real or if you're making it up. We finally hear a voice, or feel something, then immediately question it. The Spirit world hardly has a chance." Charlie said he gave up the questioning long ago and stays with a sense of wonder. I am reminded of the Fifth Key to Inner Dialog - Wonder, to keep a sense of wonder, like that of a child.

During this meeting I read three days of writings. Then we went into a meditation to see what would happen. Here is a summary, the best I can remember, of what happened. Marge put on the Music by Marcey Sampler CD. My teeth began chattering and I started feeling like I was vibrating inside so I knew Spirits were around. Also, the energy was intense, indicating the Higher Ones.

A voice came through welcoming everyone with powerful feelings of pulsing waves and a message. I don't remember the words, but we all felt it as powerful. Then I saw a round fountain filled with liquid light coming up from the center, like water would, with 10 individual streams arching up, then down into the top of each person's head. Off to my right was a doorway between me and the couch, and the Spirit Realm used it as a portal. In came about a dozen Tibetan monks. They didn't say anything, just proceeded to enter the circle, walk left around the inside of the circle and sat down chanting.

Then I saw Native Americans riding up on horses. Maybe a dozen of them. One got off and entered the circle through the doorway. He was carrying some items. He did not acknowledge the group but turned to me and proceeded to acknowledge me as Yei Bi Chai. *(See Addendum)* He gave me a robe of blue - it looked like a cape - greens to go around my neck (I was later told by someone in the group the greens are typically pine) and a Yei Bi Chai face mask.

Then he knelt and put something around my ankles. They have hurt a bit and felt heavy since. Whatever it is it feels permanently attached. He stood and said I was " One Who Speaks to the Spirits." He briefly acknowledged all within the group, then quickly turned and left the circle to get on his horse. All who were with him looked at me for a moment, then turned and rode off. I didn't recognize the tribe.

Next came elementals and fairies. I have denied them publicly in the past, thinking they were only fairy tale, and much to my chagrin they insisted I acknowledge their presence publicly - or they weren't leaving. They also wished to acknowledge themselves as partnered with the forests and other aspects of nature, but primarily with the forests. They wished it known that they are around those who are "rememberers," those who are awake. They avoid the dark places, implying polluted places and people with a lot of negativity.

Next came in the forest presence - from all around the

140

world. They wanted to be acknowledged within the circle and impressed (rather than spoke) that most trees and forests were living and awake. They also were resolute to acknowledged the elementals and fairy kingdoms - to affirm their reality in this dimension. When I acknowledged this they moved to the outside of the circle.

Next came the "Ancient Ones," referring to whales. Dolphins were with them. Charlie, said he could feel a dolphin in his hands. When I looked with my Inner Vision, I could see he was holding a baby dolphin, and a mother and another baby were close by. Charlie acknowledged that it was a small one. The dolphin stayed with him a long time.

After the antics of the dolphins, one of the Ancient Ones moved right up to me and looked at me eye to eye. It was a bit intimidating as they are quite large. Then the Ancient One merged with me, turned to face out and impressed (not spoke) that at one point we had all been Ancient Ones or the Keepers of the Sound. Now we were Land-Walkers. Then they all left.

At one point Homer came and I saw and felt him stand behind Marge. He had been transformed into Light. It was as if he had been moved into Love. It felt very big and pure. Marge felt him enter, too. She had been dowsing for his presence because he hadn't shown up right away.

Then I heard, "The Living Flame of the Heart is the burning flame that does not burn." The impression was that we could burn away all that no longer served us, including everything from disease to emotional distress. The Living Flame of the Heart is able to transmute without harm to us. We can immerse ourselves in a visualization of standing in the Living Flame of the Heart as it clears our being, yet it would not harm us. A cool flame to us, a transmuting flame to our negative aspects.

141

At the end the Tibetan monks got up, acknowledged everyone in the group and left the same way they came in. Then it was done. This is all I can remember. When we finished, many in the group reported strong Qi (energy) feelings, such as tingling, pulsing and fullness in the hands and body.

Addendum

Within weeks of moving to Tucson, I had to go to Sedona to teach a workshop. Sedona was having a festival with stores open late, crafts, music and food vendors in the street. I was looking around the Naja Gift Shop when something happened that has never happened before, or since. For a moment, I completely lost my vision and everything turned black, except for an oval of light around a blue statue of a Native American-looking man. The statue seemed to glow from behind.

In awe I said, "That belongs to me." I asked to see it and if someone could tell me what it was. I had never seen anything like it before. It was a Yei Bi Chai (pronounced yee be shay or yeah ba shay) The owner said it meant, "One Who Speaks to the Spirits to bring healing."

It was created by a local Native American artist. This fifteen-inch statue is sculpted from red clay but painted. It is a male Indian wearing a blue cape with fringe around the collar; a plain face-mask with a blunt corn pipe nose, and a large green garland neck piece.

I'm not familiar with the clothing. It looks like some kind of fabric wrap for a skirt; heavy, pointed knee boots that might be made out of fur; two strings of jewelry around the neck, and thick straps crisscrossing the chest. His hands are out in front of him looking like he should be holding something. The hair

142

is blunt cut at the bangs. The sculpture was priced at $600 but was on clearance. I couldn't afford the piece, even on clearance, but the owner of the shop knew it was mine. She sold it to me at a price that stretched me but I could afford - and less then she herself had paid for it. It was made in 1993 and never sold. In the fall of 1999, the owner put it on clearance for the festival on a whim . . . minutes before I walked into her store.

24

Homer Returns

Introduction

After seeing Homer for the last time with the Higher Ones on 25 May, I didn't think I would ever see him again. I no longer experienced the, by now, familiar "Homer buzz." I had gotten used to him being around pestering me to go in and write, so the silence was deafening. I continued some fruitful Inner Journeys with my Collective, mostly because I had committed to do so, but it wasn't as easy without Homer to bridge the gap. It took a lot more effort, energy, time, discipline and concentration to hold open the communication, but I did it anyway.

I never had time (okay, didn't take the time) to go back and look at the previous writings, because I was angry and confused about why I was being forced to do the writings. And I didn't remember what they said much after I wrote them, so all the comfort and understanding I may have felt in the moment of doing the writing didn't translate to my outer life - where I was still experiencing headaches, an occasional panic attack, and four months and more of diarrhea from the stress.

It wasn't until editing this book in the last week that I've come to appreciate the pattern and flow of the transmissions and my journey of unfoldment. While out driving the other day I realized I was really feeling pretty good about Homer & Friends in my life - but the Inner Awakening / Remembering took five months to fully integrate through three out of four of my bodies - mental, emotional and spiritual. I'm still working with physical

145

symptoms, and sometimes emotional ones. In transmissions I've received in the past two weeks I've been told my body is going through a "transmutation," what ever that means, and will be for a couple more months. We'll see.

As I'm preparing the transmissions for print I'm having to read them over and over again. I'm beginning to see what all the excitement is about them because I'm getting more out of them the more I read them. But the greatest gift for me personally has been to read about all the comfort the Spirit Realm was sending me all the while I was in such despair. If I had reread them earlier I wonder if I would have healed sooner . . . but I was too angry and confused . . . .

But before I go, I want to end *Homer's Journey* by sharing the first part of a transmission I received the morning of 2 June 2003. It is Homer's experiences about where he'd been in the eight-day period of his Transformation. For two hours and twenty minutes, I wrote until my body finally gave out, and I had to quit. It was the longest session we had ever done.

2 June 2003

Note from Ellie: I woke up early and thought I was imagining things. My teeth were chattering and my body was buzzing. "Homer?" I thought with both dread and relief. I ran to my computer and opened a new page, all the while wondering where Homer had been. I released a breath, closed my eyes and began, still intensely feeling the "Homer buzz."

E: Homer? You're back! I haven't felt you for a long time. It's been so long, I didn't think I would hear from you again.

Homer: You were told I'd be back. And I am, yet I am not the same as I was, being in the Presence of The One. I wish

146

you all to know you can come to that place and reside with the Higher Ones, even while living on the earth, because you do not live only there. You also travel to the Inner Places/Dimensions at night, however, most are so filled with lower level thinking that only the Lower Inner Dimensions are traveled to.

When you refine your Spirit and reside with higher level thinking - cultivating the FEELINGS of Inspiration, Joy, Love, Gratitude, and Wonder - then you are able to reside at the Higher Planes within. Only then will you be able to come and commune with the Higher Ones.

E: Will you share your experience? Where you've been?

Homer: It felt like only a moment, yet you say I was gone a long time. Being in the Presence (of The One) . . . . . in only that moment of existence . . . . never leaving it . . . . created pulses . . . . waves of Light and Sound . . . . that even you can feel living on the earth . . . . . if properly attuned . . . . . When residing with the Higher Ones I *became* (the) Sound and Light waves . . . . so immersed with it there was nothing else . . . time did not exist . . . . . . (everything in) space was in my consciousness. It was . . . . everything that ever was, or will be, was within me. All that was past and future was within me in that moment . . . . . . I was within it - there was no difference.

E: Did you sense others with you?

Homer: Of course. It was like singing the most beautiful song, while knowing others were singing the song too, but being in such ecstasy of the moment that every other consciousness only enhanced my own experience, bringing a greater crescendo to the piece, greater ecstasy, a greater spiritual high. There was

147

awareness of others in the form of knowing without distraction.

E: I saw you when you made the transition to be with the Higher Ones. You were very bright that day, but your presence and energy was more human-like than now. Now, you seem fuller, expanded, and bright with a fullness of power. Oh . . . . like a powerful presence with the "Homer buzz" but more "Master Teacher" like, with a Homer personality.

Homer: This weekend in your workshop you spoke of the first law of thermodynamics - that 'energy can be neither created nor destroyed, it can only be converted from one form to another.' I have been with the Higher Ones who Dance with The One, and I've been in the Dance. I am plugged into the Power Source of Creation, so energy is being redirected through me. I'm 'charged up' now. My strand of consciousness as 'Homer' is to help do these writings and other things, yet I am more plugged into the Higher Realms as my Whole Self than I am here as Homer. Everyone is, to the degree of their consciousness and their cultivation of the Five Keys to the Higher Realms of the Inner Dimensions.

E: What are they?

Homer: You can only travel to the Higher Realms through Inspiration, Joy, Love, Gratitude and Wonder. Here is a meditation to bring one to that place. First, prepare the mind, emotions and body using the Rainbow Sun Meditation previously sent through.

Ellie, you are to create the words of the meditation with ocean waves and recommend people play any *Music by Marcey* in the background while doing the meditation. It will bring

148

healing in all the lower levels and lift one up. It
healing to those who are not able to enter into medit
or are unwilling to do Eastern mystical practices that sec.
unfamiliar or complicated. Now people will be able to benefit
from the Inner Teachings and experience them in a new Western
way that can lift their Spirit and bring healing.

Rainbow Sun Meditation

Three times the Rainbow Sun washes through the body from
the top of the head, down through the body, out the feet into the
earth, where the earth recycles what you no longer need. The
first time clears the mental debris; the second time emotional
debris and the third clears all physical pain and dis-ease. The
earth recycles the stagnant energy. On the fourth descent, the
Rainbow Sun expands until you fully stand within it.

Now move your attention into your Heart Center. Begin
breathing through your heart as if you were an ocean wave . . .
. . as if you were being lifted up . . . . cresting . . . . . pausing . .
. . then down . . . . . Wave Breathing . . . . . Feel it in your body
. . . . . .

Use Wave Breathing with the FEELING of each of the Five
Keys to the Higher Realms. Begin with the feeling of Joy . . .
. breathing in JOY . . . . . as if you were being lifted up on an
ocean wave . . . . cresting . . . . . pausing . . . . then out with your
breath.

After a time breathe the FEELING of Inspiration. Continue
on with breathing Love and Laugher, Gratitude and finally
Wonder. Breathe them all in, one at a time, through the heart, and
you will naturally feel it spreading out through the whole body.
Breathing in Joy, Inspiration, Love, Gratitude and Wonder will
heal you. It will bring you into the Higher Realms.

149

This meditation, done daily, will cure all sickness for the body, mind and spirit, for there will be no dis-ease left within. There cannot be if you are SINCERE and able to fully move into these FEELINGS. This is the meditation to use with Marcey's Music. Using the image and sounds of ocean waves will also be helpful.

Now, there are others who wish to speak this morning . . . .

Afterward

It was shortly after this transmission, Homer informed me what had been written "was to be put into a book," and that we had "already begun working on the second one." I was still experiencing a great deal of stress around this whole experience so wasn't too pleased to hear that, but it also felt inevitable. I also had Marge and her monthly group, and my weekly Thursday night Circle *(where Homer first showed up)*, encouraging me in wonderfully supportive ways - sharing with me how the information was helping them personally, in addition to the people they were sharing the Homer writings with.

I had support even from my ex-husband, ("Have fun! You are so lucky to have answers and experiences people only dream about. To have access to the other side and you're stressed about this and don't want to do it? Are you crazy? I want the first copy of the book!), along with my kids, parents and grandmother who'd ask, "How's Homer? What's he talking about now?"

When people wonder how Donald (my life-partner) is handling Homer in our life, I say, "He's happy Homer wants us to do Qigong for Kids." Donald is *always* wanting to do transformational and meaningful projects for kids. Truthfully, Homer is keeping Donald nearly as busy as he is keeping me, maybe more, he's the one staying up all night doing the layout and cover design for this book . . . . and all our video production stuff . . . . and our Web site . . . . . he's our "technical guru." If Donald wasn't in my life, I don't think any of the Homer information would have ever gotten done.

The greatest gift Donald has given me, however, is to not look at me like I'm crazy when I walk into his office and say something like, "I've just been told we need to do such and such for the project," and it's obvious someone from the Spirit Realm has been talking to me. He has been wonderful throughout it all - even practical. One day as I was lying in bed with him crying about all these Spirits trying to talk to me he simply said, "You'll get over it." I wanted to hit him. How Donald came into my life is another story about Spirit interfering . . . . . I stubbornly resisted that time too now that I'm thinking about it . . . . . and now I can't imagine my life without him.

My Astrology Consultant, Jeff Linzer, *(See Addendum)* was also a big support, but in a different way. Throughout the year, he had been keeping in contact with me about the "big changes" I might be going through, letting me know what planets were where and how I *might* experience the effects of their energies.

In other years he'd maybe call me twice to let me know things were going on. This year Jeff called me more times than in the previous ten years we've worked together! (The second most was the year I divorced, moved to Tucson with my ex-husband, went to China and met Donald.) I remember him saying it would be as momentous as my 1999 transformation, but my life was great so I couldn't imagine what would change. How could I have ever known?

Astrologically speaking, there were numerous planets all making life-changing shifts. In my chart many of them happened to be doing it all at once and in ways that were making me particularly sensitive (psychic). "2003 will be a year of big changes and graduations." "You're life won't be the same." "Respect the energies coming in, because some of them may be challenging, but you'll do fine. Astrological influences create only opportunities for you to be more of who you are, anyway." Looking back, could I say it had been *foretold*? The heavens *foretold* Homer coming into my life? Or did these astrological shifts of energy create an opening and Homer found it?

By the middle of July, Brian and Maggie Disbury, a British couple who live in Tucson, had been to a dowser's conference in California. They had brought their photocopies of the Homer writings with them. Upon their return from the conference we had a meeting at Marge's and Brian could hardly wait to speak with me. *(Brian and Maggie had been attending the monthly meetings at Marge's home. Brian introduced Homer at the beginning of this book.)*

As soon as I walked in the door, Brian began telling me how excited people in California were to see the writings. But . . . they didn't want me to change a thing - they'd rather have photocopies of the originals than any "doctored up book that was so perfect the life would be sucked out of it."

Brian was telling me this because I had already sent the Homer writings off to my editor in Phoenix; Brian knew I had told the editor to "take out all my pathetic musings" about "doubt, and none of it being real," which would have eliminated most of the "Notes from Ellie." Brian and Maggie insisted the doubts were what made it real; it was what the people in California liked the best. It was raw and imperfect - more like real life. Everyone in the Sunday group strongly agreed with this, so I promised I would call the editor immediately and have her put everything back in and to leave the writings intact, and

152

in the order I had originally received them.

Thank goodness for Lilliana Edwards. She didn't even miss a beat, used to the creative process, "No problem. I'll add a few things back in." Lilly and I met last summer before I went to Tibet and became fast friends; as if we'd known each other a lifetime. Upon first meeting her (on the phone) she said something like, "Spirit said I was supposed to call you, but I had to test you out first before I shared that."

What I didn't know at the time was that she had been a law professor and had written and edited text books, and is one of the most brilliant and creative people I know. When this project came up she enthusiastically volunteered to do the editing, and she let me be creative! Lilly is also one of the few people I know who spends as much time communicating with Spirit as I do. Who better to edit this work when she so clearly understood the messages and process. It was an amazing coincidence. Spirit at work again?

In August, Brian and Maggie planned to attend the British Society of Dowser's 70th Anniversary Congress in Manchester (England) and they wanted to take books with them. That Sunday in July, I sat there with ten people looking at me with anticipation. "Okay . . . . I can try to get it done, but I don't know if I can on time. I don't even know what to charge for it!"

Spontaneously, ten dowsers reached into their pockets (or purses) for their pendulums and immediately started dowsing the price. I think I fell in love with everyone of them right then. It was a precious moment I will never forget and very funny. None of them even thought about it - they just went for their pendulums.

In that same gathering, Virginia Moyer, an artist and dowser in the group, came over and quietly said she had been dreaming about Homer and had started a painting, trying to capture the dream. The style of the painting was different than how she usually worked. She hadn't finished it yet, but said if it worked as cover art for the book, she would like to donate it. Ginny gave it to me four days later (actually two paintings, equally beautiful). It is the artwork you see on the cover.

I was unable to complete the book for Brian and Maggie to take with them to England. Instead I created a seven-page introduction so they could have something on paper to share. When they got back Brian let me know, "We attended the British Society of Dowsers (BSD) Congress and they were interested enough in 'The Homer Connection' to post the seven pages on the conference notice-board for people to read." Also, that "Pauline Roberts, an Australian from New South Wales and current editor of the BSD Journal, was very interested." It appears *Homer's Journey* may be going out to the other side of the world soon.

I am humbled by the many wonderful people who have generously given their time, talents and resources to make *Homer's Journey* possible. I am grateful, beyond words, for the emotional support I've received from so many during my hours of despair. I couldn't have done it without you. Thank you, a thousand times, thank you . . . . from both of us.

Addendum

I know I'm going to get requests about how to contact Jeff so I will include it here if you are interested: Jeff Linzer's Down to Earth Astrology contact information is 612-924-0946 or jefflinzerastro@earthlink.net. If it ever changes we'll post it on the Web site. Jeff is in Minnesota but does readings all over the country via the phone.

154

It's been great for me since I moved to Tucson! Especially this year. I'm taking all the support I can get. I wonder what next year is going to look like? By the way, his wife Cindy, is probably one of the most talented sensitives I know. Both are down to earth, humble, great folks, and I'm glad they are part of my life. I am in awe for how much I have to be thankful for!